# Multicurrency in QuickBooks® Desktop

Esther Friedberg Karp, MBA

# Contents

## Module 1: What You Need to Know before Turning on Multicurrency in QuickBooks Desktop

## Module 2: Foreign Currency Transactions and Exchange Gains and Losses

# Module 3: Foreign Currency Transactions in QuickBooks Desktop - Beyond the Basics

## Module 4: Multicurrency Reporting & Troubleshooting in QuickBooks Desktop

# Module 1: What You Need to Know before Turning on Multicurrency in QuickBooks Desktop

# Chapter 1
# Introduction to Multicurrency and QuickBooks Desktop

## About This book

This book will guide you through the functionality of using QuickBooks Desktop to track foreign currency transactions and balances for you. For the purposes of this book, every mention of QuickBooks will refer to QuickBooks Desktop (unless Quick-Books Online is named).

Optionally, you can purchase a practice company file from our website, complete with real dates and exchange rates. You will see instructions in chapter 5. Use only the data file intended for the country's version of QuickBooks that you are using. Depending on your version year or if you're using QuickBooks Enterprise, the data file may have to be upgraded; always download and keep a copy of these original portable files.

In most situations, you can use any edition of QuickBooks Desktop in a Multicurrency situation: Pro, Premier, or Enterprise. There is one situation where having Pro isn't quite enough, and that's when using foreign price levels. We'll cover all that later in the book.

## About Multicurrency in QuickBooks Desktop

Multicurrency can be enabled in any Windows version of QuickBooks, including Pro. However, if you wish to maintain any foreign price lists, you'll need QuickBooks Premier (available in the US, Canada, and, until January 31, 2023, in the UK) or Enterprise (available in the US and Canada).

There is no limit to the number of currencies you can track using QuickBooks Desktop and Multicurrency. As long as a currency exists for a country on Planet Earth, it's available to be tracked in QuickBooks. Some obscure currencies for smaller countries would require the exchange rates to be entered manually. As far as cryptocurrencies are concerned, Bitcoin is the only one at this time that is allowed, but its exchange rates have to be entered manually.

## For QuickBooks Mac Users in the US

Multicurrency is not supported in QuickBooks for Mac US (and there is no Canadian or UK Mac version). If you need QuickBooks multicurrency functionality and you are using a Mac, you have four choices to continue with the same company file you've been using for some time, and they all start with converting the Mac data to QuickBooks for Windows. You can convert your Mac data to QuickBooks for Windows and then do one of the following:

1. Access that converted data in QuickBooks for Windows in a Windows emulator on your Mac;
2. Access that converted data in a cloud-hosted instance of QuickBooks for Windows;
3. Access that converted data in a server-installed instance of QuickBooks for Windows;

4. Convert the QuickBooks for Windows data to QuickBooks Online (Essentials or higher to start using multicurrency).

- In this case, you'll be opening the Windows data only temporarily on a Windows-based machine (or any of the options 1-3 above) and won't need a full license of QuickBooks for Windows. A trial will do, and you can download trial versions of QuickBooks Desktop here: https://downloads.quickbooks.com/app/qbdt/products.
- Just select **Get a trial version** in the top right corner and then **QuickBooks Desktop – United States**

Be aware that conversions from QuickBooks Mac to QuickBooks Windows do not always run smoothly; there are restrictions and you run the risk of corruption. There are limitations in the QuickBooks Mac product compared to its Windows counterparts, and you might have to clean up the Mac data first. Consult the Intuit website for more information on converting Mac files to Windows.

Here are two Knowledge Base articles from Intuit that can get you started:

https://quickbooks.intuit.com/learn-support/en-us/update-products/convert-a-quickbooks-for-mac-file-to-quickbooks-for-windows/00/186463

https://quickbooks.intuit.com/learn-support/en-us/do-more-with-quickbooks/community-questions-converting-quickbooks-desktop-windows-and/00/153822

Of course, you can, at any time, visit https://quickbooks.intuit.com/learn-support/ and search for the string *convert Mac to Windows*.

# Chapter 2
# Why You Need Multicurrency (and Why You Might Not)

## Do You Need Multicurrency?

It's important to note that turning on Multicurrency changes the database supporting your QuickBooks working file, and it cannot be undone. So be sure that Multicurrency is indeed what your company needs. QuickBooks recommends making a backup of your Desktop company file before doing something permanent like turning on Multicurrency, and I wholeheartedly agree.

Having said that, you might actually need to track multiple currencies for your company. Here are a couple of qualifying questions to ask yourself:

1. Do you transact with foreign currency customers and/or vendors in their own currency (but foreign currency as far as you're concerned) on a regular basis?
2. Do you maintain accounts and their balances in other currencies? These include bank accounts, credit card accounts, accounts payable (for tracking foreign vendor bills), and accounts receivable (for tracking foreign customer invoices).

If you answered "yes" to either of these two questions, you are a good candidate for using multicurrency in QuickBooks.

## Why You Might Not Need Multicurrency

If you don't maintain foreign bank, credit card, accounts payable or accounts receivable accounts, it's likely that you don't need multicurrency. That occasional software purchase from a company in a different country on your home country's credit card doesn't make you a multicurrency candidate. Not at all. These transactions are translated by the credit card company to your domestic currency. Turning on multicurrency for that kind of scenario would be like "killing an ant with an elephant gun." And unless you've backed up the "ant" (your QuickBooks Desktop company file), you should use it without multicurrency turned on.

There are features in QuickBooks Desktop that do not work once multicurrency is enabled, and still others that continue to work but not with foreign currency transactions. It's important to know what you'll continue to access in QuickBooks and what you won't after you've enabled multiple currencies.

In addition, if the QuickBooks file has been used for some time without multicurrency enabled, and you have employed workarounds to handle foreign currency transactions, you should know something else. All existing names on the Chart of Accounts, Customer List and Vendor List that were in place prior to turning on multicurrency are assigned the home currency (the one in which you run reports and file your financials with your government). Then there would be extra work required to create new foreign accounts and names and move transactions and/or balances from the old names to the new names.

For more information, refer to the material on *What Happens When You Turn on Multicurrency* and *What if You were Tracking Foreign Currencies Before Turning on Multicurrency?*

## Fraud Risk

I've seen business owners be defrauded by unscrupulous employees who had access to QuickBooks over the years. A chunk of these had to do with the gain/loss on foreign exchange, whether multicurrency was turned on or not.

Here is a word of caution: if you are going to track foreign currency transactions and balances in QuickBooks, make sure you and the other users understand what QuickBooks does. More importantly, make sure you understand what the various QuickBooks users are doing, as I've seen my share of employees sweep mistakes and fraudulent transactions under the *foreign exchange gain or loss* rug.

# Chapter 3
# Risks of Dealing in Multiple Currencies

Dealing in more than one currency is more than just a matter of pinpointing what the selling price should be for your goods and services in other countries' units of money. It involves a great deal of risk and uncertainty because exchange rates (the number of currency A units it takes to equal a unit of currency B) fluctuate, and so they can affect both your sales and your expenses. Exchange gain or loss can even move your company from black ink to red.

## This is how risky foreign currencies can be

Let's take an historical example. Let's say your company is located in the United States, and therefore your domestic or home currency is the US Dollar, because you report and file taxes to your country's governing authority (e.g. the IRS) and therefore you are using the United States currency.

The US dollar (USD) reached a *high* vs. the Canadian dollar (CAD) on January 18, 2002. On that date:

1 CAD was worth 0.6199 USD
1 USD was worth 1.6132 CAD

*(Note: these rates are reciprocals of each other.)*

The US dollar (USD) reached a *low* vs. the Canadian dollar (CAD) on November 7, 2007. On that date:

> 1 CAD was worth 1.0905 USD
> 1 USD was worth 0.9170 CAD

*(Again, when you're dealing with the exchange rate between two currencies A and B, the exchange rate of currency B expressed in the number of currency A units is the reciprocal of the exchange rate of currency A expressed in the number of currency B units.)*

Further to that, let's say you're buying an essential widget for your company from the only vendor on the planet, a company based in Canada.

If you bought a widget in January 2002 from this Canadian vendor, and it cost you $1 USD at the time, what would it cost you to buy that same widget in November 2007, even if there was no price change or inflation? You may be surprised by the answer:

> $1.76

If you're shocked and in disbelief, here's the math:

In January, 2002, you bought a widget that cost you $1 USD, which, at the time, was the equivalent of $1.6132 CAD, so that's the real price of the widget in its country's currency. If there was no price change or inflation on that price in CAD, you'd have to pay the Canadian vendor the USD equivalent of that static price in November, 2007. But at that time, the CAD was worth 1.0905 USD. So, in order to come up with the equivalent of that price in USD, you'd have to take that price and multiply it by the exchange rate: $1.6132 CAD x 1.0905 USD/CAD = $1.7592 USD.

So our much-needed widget is 76% more expensive just based on exchange rate swings alone, even if the original Canadian (i.e. the foreign) price is unchanged. And, in the real world, prices do change, and banks, credit cards, and payment processors also charge a premium over the exchange rate. So if this were a real situation with these dates and rates, the fluctuation can be even greater than 76%.

If this widget is an essential input to the goods or services that you sell, you need to make sure that the selling price of those goods or services is high enough to keep it profitable. And, as you likely know, changing a selling price can have an impact on the demand for it, especially if you have competitors that undercut you. If you don't track exchange rate swings and their impact on your sales and expenses, you might be operating at a loss and not know it until it's too late to change your prices or your offerings. When it's too late, you might have to close your business.

## What if I want to avoid foreign currency altogether?

You might say to yourself: *"I'll institute a policy that I will only deal in my own currency; that way, I'm not experiencing foreign currency risks."*

That policy won't get you anywhere. In fact, it can prevent your business from growing and you can lose ground to your competition.

And here's why: that Canadian vendor might feel the same way as you do, and won't provide you with a fixed USD price for their widgets. And if you're selling to customers all over the world, *they* want to know what your goods and services are really going to cost *them* in their own currency. The international shopping climate is such that people shy away from prices that are not quoted in their own currency; they want to know the real cost to them in their own currency. If you look at surveys of online shoppers, you'll see "hidden or unexpected extra costs," "prices are too high," and "price presented in foreign currency" as prominent reasons global respondents cited for abandoning their digital shopping carts. So it makes sense to offer customers pricing in their own currency.

## What if I enter all foreign currency transactions as if they're priced in my currency?

Here's a disastrous situation I've seen many times over the years. Let's take a US company that makes purchases from vendors and sales to customers based in Canada, Europe, and Japan. All euro, CAD, and yen transactions are entered as if they're denominated in USD...or in other words, as if each of those foreign currencies is at *par* with the US dollar. The only way they differentiate among transactions in the various currencies is by adding a label (e.g. "SmithCo - CAD" as the name of a Canadian customer or using the account name "Sales - CAD" on the Profit & Loss).

A transaction of 100 Japanese yen, for example, would be counted by your bookkeeping system as if it were worth $100 USD, instead of less than $1 USD, which it is worth as of the time of the creation of this lesson.

While following this practice is certainly simpler than dealing with exchange rates, it leads directly to confusion, as well as incorrect numbers and financials. All reports would be taken with a grain of salt, and would not be "ready for prime time" unless they were exported to Excel (and every transaction or balance would be multiplied by an agreed-upon exchange rate that was considered to be effective over the period of time reflected in the report).

Further, you would have a very long chart of accounts, as you'd need different income, cost of goods sold, and expense accounts for each currency. Systems like this are very fragile indeed; with all the similarly-named accounts, it's very easy to make a mistake when categorizing transactions. Then a 100 yen income transaction (worth under $1 USD) could mistakenly be entered as a 100 euro income transaction (worth over $110 USD as of the writing of this lesson). It would take hours and hours to produce financial statements taking all the different currencies into account, and their accuracy would be suspect indeed.

## What other "gotchas" should I look out for when using multicurrency?

It's really important to understand the meaning and ramifications of foreign currency transactions. This is important whether you're a business owner/user or an accounting professional supporting clients with foreign transactions.

It's not just a matter of getting a true picture of profitability or loss, which is obviously vital. It's also a matter of many people not understanding multicurrency but they're afraid to admit it. Think of Hans Christian Andersen's story "The Emperor's New Clothes." No one wanted to admit they couldn't see the new clothes for fear that they would be viewed as stupid. The same is true of multicurrency; few understand it, but of those that don't understand it, *very few* will admit to it.

As a result, people with access to QuickBooks who have something to hide will often sweep a lot of garbage entries under the Exchange Gain or Loss account rug, knowing full well that people won't look into that account because they don't know what it means. In other words, untrustworthy staff consider the Exchange Gain or Loss account a fantastic place to hide fraud.

We'll cover what should and should not be in this account later on in this book.

# Chapter 4
# What Happens When you Turn on Multicurrency

When you turn on Multicurrency in a QuickBooks data file, changes are made to the company file. Turning on Multicurrency is **irreversible**. So if you're not sure if you should turn on multicurrency, I've got a couple of suggestions for you.

The first suggestion is to create a copy of your working file, name it something distinct in terms of the file name (such as "EstherCo test MC file YYMMDD.qbw") as well as in terms of the Company name in the My Company / Company Information). You might also go into **Edit > Preferences > Desktop View** and change the color scheme of this company so that at a glance, it's *very* different from your current working file. If you're in a network environment, I suggest you put this test company on your desktop so no one else sees it. If you're using Attachments or Logos in your forms, this copied and re-named file will not maintain a connection to your Attachments and Images folders, but it's fine for testing purposes.

The other suggestion is offered up by QuickBooks itself: When you start to turn on Multiple Currencies in a company file, you'll see a warning pop-up window such as this one appear. Take heed as to what won't work anymore. Most importantly, the second bullet says you should make sure you create a backup before turning on this feature. It doesn't force you to make a backup, so you should click on **No** and make the backup before you come back and proceed with the change to multicurrency.

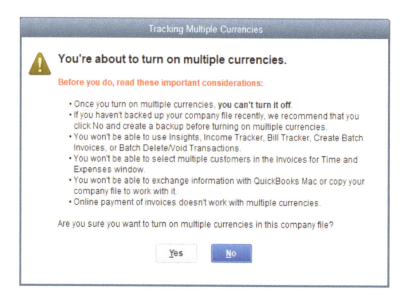

## What won't I be able to access in QuickBooks after Multicurrency is enabled?

So here's what you won't have access to when you turn on Multi-currency in QuickBooks Desktop:

- Insights on the Home Page
- Income Tracker
- Bill Tracker
- Create Batch Invoices
- Batch Delete / Void Transactions
- Can't select multiple customers in Invoices for Time and Expenses window
- Can't exchange information with QuickBooks for Mac
- Online payment of invoices doesn't work with multiple currencies

This is just a list of the main features that change. Another thing that changes is this: if you're tracking billable time, and even if you've set up foreign pricing for this billable time's service item, here's what happens. When you bring billable time over to an invoice, you'll see the home or domestic price  for this item converted into the foreign price at whatever the prevailing exchange rate is on that date. In other words, the foreign pricing you've set up for this service item will not appear; instead, you'll see the domestic price you've set up for this item converted into the foreign currency at that day's exchange rate. You'll need to overwrite this figure. We'll cover this in more detail in a later lesson.

## How will the QuickBooks company file change?

Besides what you won't have access to anymore, here's how your company file will change after Multicurrency is turned on:

- Multicurrency cannot be turned off
- New list called *Currency List*
- Select currencies you want to see and download or create exchange rates manually
- A new account (*Other Expense* type) will appear on the Chart of Accounts: *Exchange Gain or Loss.* It will only appear the first time QuickBooks calculates and records a gain or loss on foreign exchange.
- All pre-existing general ledger accounts, vendors, and customers are assigned the home currency (most often, it's your country's currency)
- All pre-existing transactions are in the home currency
- All new bank accounts, credit card accounts, customers, and vendors can be assigned a foreign currency
- Just remember that if you assign a currency to a customer or vendor, you can only conduct transactions with that name in that currency. If you have a customer

or vendor with whom you deal in more than one
currency, you'd need to create a name for that customer
or vendor for each currency, for example:

- *Smith, John (USD)* for all USD transactions
- *Smith, John (euro)* for all euro transactions

We'll cover this in more detail later in this book.

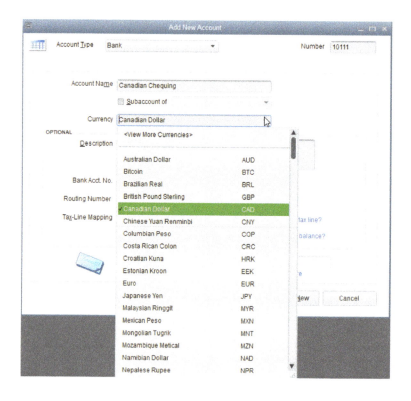

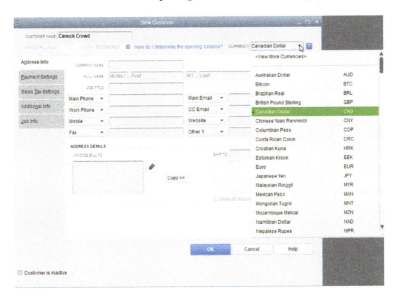

- You'll see a currency column in the Chart of Accounts, as well as the Customer Center and the Vendor Center
- Balances on the Chart of Accounts are denominated in whatever an account's currency is. If an Australian-denominated bank account appears on the Chart of Accounts with a balance of 3225.81, that's in Australian dollars.
- New field on transactions for the currency's exchange rate
- Can't create an exchange rate between two foreign currencies - but there is a workaround that we'll cover later in this book
- If you have several different Accounts Receivable accounts, QuickBooks Desktop will allow you to maintain different invoice number sequences for each of them. So the Canadian A/R account can have all invoices starting with CAD-001, CAD-002, and so on. The Euro A/R account can have all invoices starting with EUR-001, EUR-002, and so on.

- Billable time tracked for foreign currency customer - service item comes over at the home currency price converted to the foreign currency at that date's prevailing exchange rate: you'll need to overwrite the foreign price
- This happens even if you've set up foreign pricing for this billable time's service item
- Refer to the lesson *Foreign Currency: Miscellaneous Items to Consider* in the last module
- Monetary figures on printed forms will be preceded by a currency symbol, even if it's your home currency (e.g. "USD 1,000.00")
- Payroll cannot be run from a non-home currency bank
- Currency of a new name or account can be changed if there are no transactions using that name or if it's not linked to anything else
- If you are using any third party apps that integrate with QuickBooks, make sure they can work in a Multicurrency environment
- Once you select the home currency, it cannot be changed
- If you select a home currency other than the country of QuickBooks Desktop (for example, you're using QuickBooks Desktop US and you choose the Euro as your home currency when you turn on Multicurrency), the following will occur:
- Payroll won't work
- QuickBooks Payments, if you have them enabled, won't work
- There may be odd interactions with third party applications
- Bank Feeds won't find your bank
- The Download Exchange Rates feature won't work; exchange rates must be updated manually

- The company file will grow to be larger and more complex than it otherwise would be, as it has to track foreign amounts and their home currency equivalents, as well as the exchange rates entered over time. You should verify your company file more often than you did before turning on this feature, as Multicurrency companies can fall victim to data corruption more easily than regular companies.

## Which version of QuickBooks Desktop should I use?

In most situations, you can use any edition of QuickBooks Desktop in a Multicurrency situation: Pro, Premier, or Enterprise. There is one situation where having Pro isn't quite enough, and that's when using foreign price levels. We'll cover that later in the book.

## You can still convert to QuickBooks Online

Depending on where you look online, you might see a warning that Multicurrency Desktop files cannot be converted to QuickBooks Online. While this was true once upon a time, that is no longer the case. Multicurrency QuickBooks Desktop files (for a particular country, such as QuickBooks Desktop US) can be converted to QuickBooks Online for that same country (in this case, QuickBooks Online US). Just as with non-multicurrency files, this is true as long as the number of targets of the Desktop company file does not exceed 750,000.

There are two caveats to this, though.

Firstly...you must be extra vigilant when converting Multicurrency Desktop files to QuickBooks Online. The automatic conversion utility has some funkiness to it when it comes to foreign currencies. Therefore, you should take extra care when comparing financials in both systems post-conversion. If you find differences, compare financials for earlier periods until you see where the discrepancies start. You may have to zero in on converted foreign currency transactions as they appear in Quick-Books Online and edit the exchange rate to match the rate for the corresponding transaction in Desktop. That is not true for all foreign currency transactions. You might find no issue at all, or you might find it in a handful of transactions.

The second caveat is this: QuickBooks Online calculates exchange gains and losses differently from how QuickBooks Desktop does. We will cover this in our next book, which is Multicurrency in QuickBooks Online.

## What if I already have foreign balances on my balance sheet?

Refer to the lesson *Foreign Currency: Miscellaneous Items to Consider* in the last module for more information if you have foreign balances on your balance sheet from before you turned on Multicurrency.

# Chapter 5
# Download the Demo Company for your Country (Optional)

Depending on your country's version of QuickBooks Desktop, you can choose to purchase a demo company in portable (*.QBM) company file that will work with your version. You would then restore it in your version of QuickBooks Desktop.

**Unlike the sample companies that come with QuickBooks Desktop, these files have real dates and you can download real exchange rates.**

Demo companies are available for purchase here.

*Caution: NEVER install more than one country's version of QuickBooks Desktop on the same machine. For example, do not install QuickBooks Desktop Pro, Premier, or Enterprise Canada on the same machine on which QuickBooks Desktop Pro, Premier, or Enterprise US is already installed.*

These files were created in QuickBooks Desktop 2019, so they can be restored into QuickBooks Desktop Pro, Premier, or Enterprise version year 2019 or later.

- Demo US company for using Multicurrency (Portable).QBM (company name: Rock Castle Construction, company file color scheme blue-gray)
- Demo CA company for using Multicurrency (Portable).QBM (company name: Pro Hockey School, company file colour scheme pink)

As with restoring any portable company file, you must enter the Admin user password. The credentials for both portable files are as follows:

Admin password: *Admin123*
Name of high school: *CHAT*

If you are using a newer version than 2019, you will be prompted to update the company file to your current version year as part of the restore process:

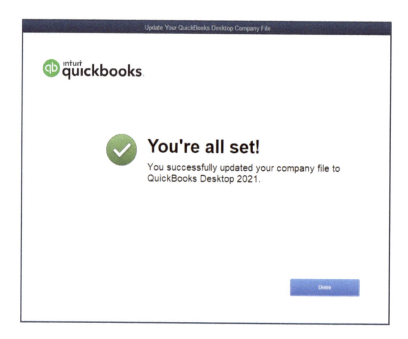

Keep the portable file you've selected someplace safe, or download it any time you use it.

As you follow along in the lessons, you may want to go back to the beginning and start with a fresh company file. If you wish to restore the portable file to the same folder on your computer more than once, you have two choices:

- Restore the portable file again and again, using the same (*.QBW) working file name. If you attempt to do that, you'll see a message indicating that the working file is read-only. In that case, **right-click on the pre-existing *.QBW file** you're trying to overwrite with the restored portable company and choose **Properties**. In the *General* tab, un-check the box next to *Read-only* and then click **OK.** Then continue to restore the company to the same working file name.

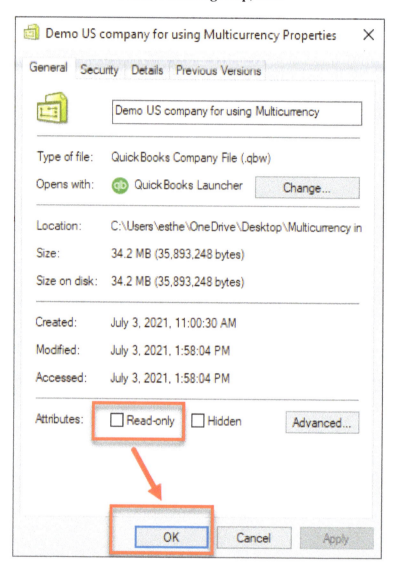

- Restore the portable company to another name altogether so you'll have more than one company demo file.

*Note to Canadian company users:* when you restore the company file, you will likely see a message that the tax table is out of date.

Ignore it. Or click on **Edit > Preferences > Payroll & Employees > Company Preferences > No Payroll**. That will turn off payroll and make this message go away.

The demonstrations will be conducted using QuickBooks Desktop Premier US.

## Chapter 6
# Download a Trial Version of QuickBooks Desktop (Optional)

If you don't have a purchased copy of QuickBooks Pro, Premier, or Enterprise in version year 2019 or later, download a 30-day trial of your country's version to test it out.

Visit this site: https://downloads.quickbooks.com/app/qbdt/ products and select **Get a trial version** in the top right corner. Then select your **country** from the drop-down to get a 30-day trial (Premier at the very least is recommended in order to follow the lesson on foreign price lists).

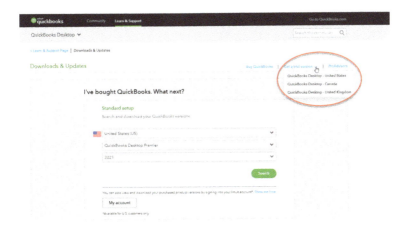

Before you download the 30-day trial, make sure your country's flag is displayed in the top right corner of the page) and restore the demo company using that software.

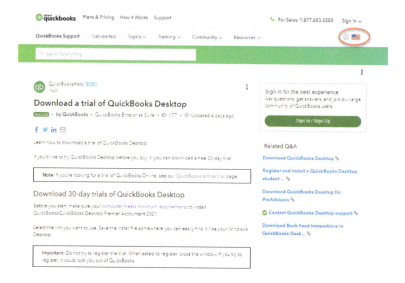

If you don't know if your computer has the appropriate system requirements to run QuickBooks Desktop, Google "quickbooks desktop system requirements" to see what the absolute minimum requirements are.

# Chapter 7
# Preparing to Turn on Multicurrency - What you Need to Know

## Verify (and rebuild if necessary) your data

Before making any major changes to your company file, it's important to verify it. If there are any problems with the company file, perform a rebuild and make any necessary changes. Verify again until you see a message that there are no problems detected.

## Back up!

After your company has been verified that there are no problems with the data, back up your data. This is standard procedure before making any major changes that cannot be reversed. That way, you can restore the backup if you're not happy with your choice of turning on Multicurrency.

You can also take a straight copy of the company or make a portable copy instead.

## Sign in as Admin user in single-user mode

As turning on Multicurrency is a Company preference, you must be signed in to the company as the Admin user in single-user mode to turn it on.

# Chapter 8
# Turn on Multicurrency

Let's take a look at the "before and after" of turning on Multicurrency in QuickBooks.

So we are logged in as the Admin user in single-user mode to a non-multicurrency company. We've already done a verify, and if necessary, a rebuild. We've also backed up, created a portable copy, or made a copy of the company in case we want to change our minds.

I've already changed the company information so that it reflects that this is a Demo for Multicurrency purposes.

The file size, which I can get by hitting **F2** on my keyboard, is 36,180K.

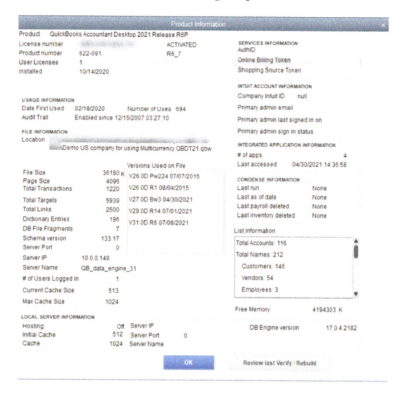

- Select **Edit** > **Preferences** > **Multiple Currencies** > **Company Preferences**.
- Select the radio button next to **Yes, I use more than one currency**.

- A window pops up with the warning *You're about to turn on multiple currencies.* Read the list of considerations, and, if you're sure you want to turn it on, after the question *Are you sure you want to turn on multiple currencies in this company file?* select **Yes**.

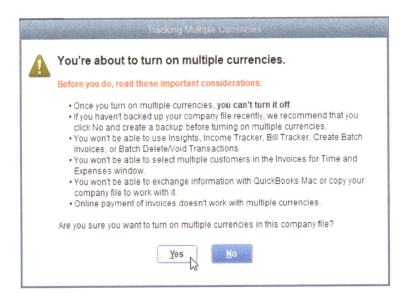

- Back in the *Company Preferences* tab, you must select
  the home or domestic currency you want to use for this
  company. This is the currency in which you would be
  reporting financials to the government. Most of the
  time, you'll leave the default selection as-is (US Dollar
  for QuickBooks Desktop US, and Canadian Dollar for
  QuickBooks Desktop Canada). There might be times
  when you would choose another country's currency as
  the home currency. We'll cover that in a later lesson.
- At any time until now, you can select **Cancel** and your
  company file will be unchanged. But if you want to go
  ahead, select **OK** and after this you cannot go back
  without restoring a backup or portable company, or
  opening a copy of the file.

- You'll see a warning window appear telling you Your
  company file will now close and reopen with your
  updated settings. Click **OK**.

> **Warning**
>
> ⚠ Your company file will now close and reopen with your updated settings.
>
> [ **OK** ]

- You'll see a working message telling you that QuickBooks is setting up the company file to work with multiple currencies. Please wait while this is setup for you. Depending on the size of your company file, this may take a few minutes.

> **Working**
>
> QuickBooks is setting up your company file to work with multiple currencies. Please wait while this is setup for you. Depending on the size of your company file, this may take a few minutes.

- The company file reopens. Take a look at the changes:
- The company file has grown (from 36,180K to 46,876K) simply by virtue of turning on Multicurrency. That's because there are new fields for exchange rates and currencies on all pre-existing transactions, even though all those transactions are recorded in what is now considered the home currency:

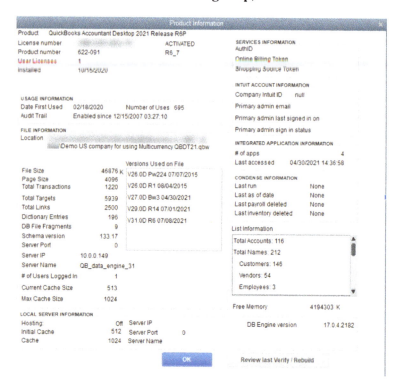

- The Chart of Accounts has a new Currency column. All accounts that were in existence before the change are assigned the home currency.

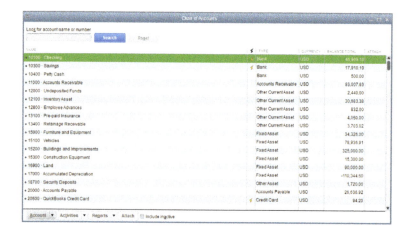

- The Chart of Accounts will also have a new account, an Other Expense account called *Exchange Gain or Loss.* This account will only appear once a gain or loss on foreign exchange has been calculated and recorded by the software.
- All the vendors and customers that existed in the file before the change are also assigned the home currency.
- Under Lists, you'll see the Currency List, which was not there before.

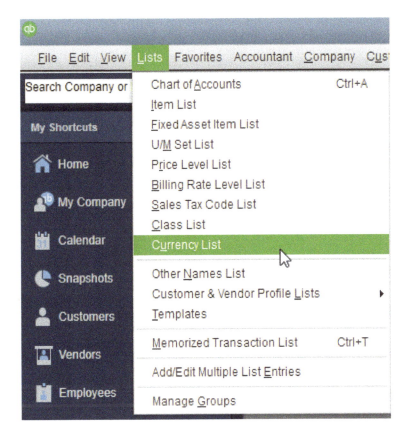

- Every transaction, even the ones that were in existence before the change, is now assigned a currency as well as an exchange rate between that currency and the home currency on the date of that transaction. Of course, since all pre-existing transactions are in the home currency, the exchange rate on all of these is 1, or par. The par exchange rate on home currency transactions cannot be edited, but foreign currency transactions, as you'll see soon, can have the exchange rate changed. You can see the new field for the currency and the exchange rate on all transactions. If this were a foreign currency transaction, we'd see the foreign amount as well as its value in the home currency at the exchange rate.

You'll also soon see that you can display the foreign amounts for a transaction in addition to the home currency debits and credits on the behind-the-scenes transaction journal.

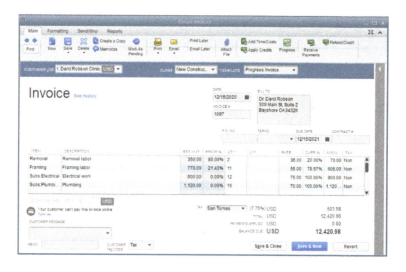

- Under the *Company* menu, you'll see a new option: *Manage Currencies*. That opens up a sub-menu including various Multicurrency functions, including another access point for the *Currency List*, *Currency Calculator* , *Download Latest Exchange Rates*, and *Home Currency Adjustment* (we'll cover those later). The Multicurrency resources, sadly, are of no use at this time.

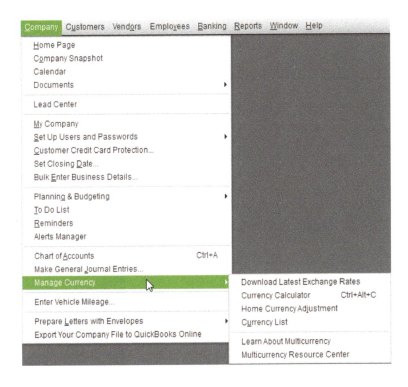

- There is one more step you need to take once Multicurrency is enabled...you must start using the Currency List to update exchange rates, either automatically or manually. If we look at the Currency List, we'll see the currencies, but no exchange rates, which means that QuickBooks will think each currency is valued exactly the same as your home currency.

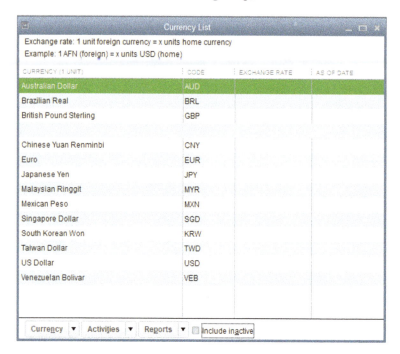

- You can remedy this quickly by selecting **Download Latest Exchange Rates**. It's available either from the **Company > Manage Currency** menu or the **Lists > Currency List** screen by selecting the **Activities** button at the bottom.

# Multicurrency in QuickBooks® Desktop

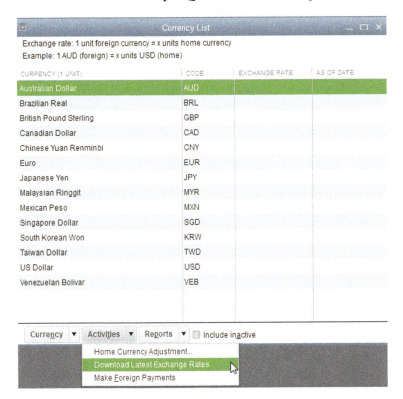

Or

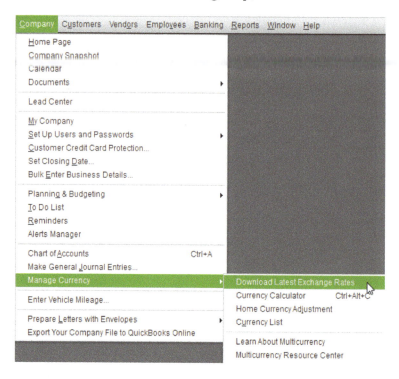

You'll see this confirmation screen. Select **OK**.

- The next time you open the Currency List, you'll see rates as of the most recent date on which you performed the download (i.e. today):

## Multicurrency in QuickBooks® Desktop

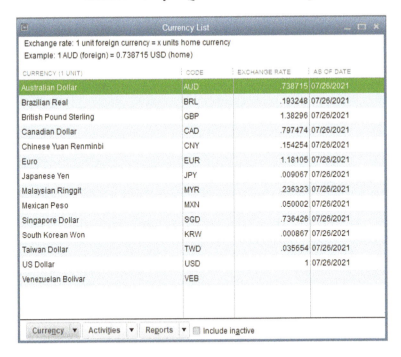

We've briefly mentioned currencies and exchange rates. Now let's see what those concepts mean.

# Chapter 9
# Currencies and Exchange Rates

### What are currencies?

Currencies are usually issued by a country's government and are generally the accepted form of monetary payment for that country.

QuickBooks Desktop allows you to track foreign currency transactions, exchange rates, as well as exchange rate gains and losses for all countries' currencies in the world.

In addition to currencies issued by countries' governments, there are digital currencies.

Digital or cryptocurrency such as Bitcoin cannot be tracked automatically in QuickBooks Desktop. (Bitcoin *does* get tracked in QuickBooks Online, though.) You can, however, create a new ("custom") currency for other uses such as digital currency or obscure currencies that QuickBooks have on its list of currencies to track (such as the South Sudanese Pound). Click on **Currency > New** and enter the currency name and 3-letter code (this should be unique; two or more currencies cannot share a code). However, you'll need to enter and update its exchange rates over time manually. And, should Bitcoin be worth more than

99,999.99 of your home currency, QuickBooks Desktop will no longer be able to accommodate an exchange rate showing decimals. Generally, exchange rates display 6 digits including decimals. However, QuickBooks Desktop can accommodate wildly large exchange rates well beyond 6 digits but it will not capture any decimals on those rates:

In this example, the Bitcoin exchange rate for July 1 was entered as 99,999.99 but QuickBooks saved it as 100,000 with no decimals. The exchange rate for July 25 captures many more digits than 6, and again, no decimals.

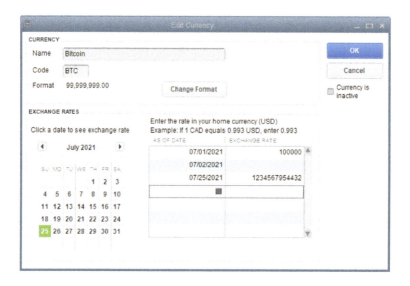

In fact, you can select **Currency > New** for any obscure (or test) currency that does not appear on the Currency list. For example, if you were doing business with Italian Bank Banco Emiliano, they allow Parmigiano-Reggiano cheese as currency in certain situations. So you would create a new currency, perhaps with the code PRC. The only caveat is that you must enter and update the exchange rates for Parmigiano-Reggiano manually, as opposed to downloading the latest exchange rates, which we'll cover later in this lesson.

As you can see in the Currency list, the exchange rate is defined as the number of home currency units you need to equal one foreign currency unit. So if a foreign currency is worth more than your home currency, the exchange rate will be greater than 1.

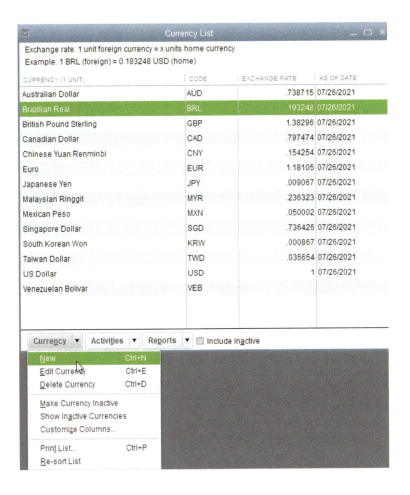

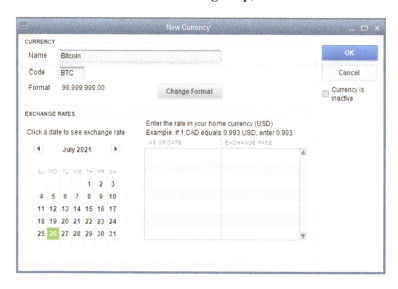

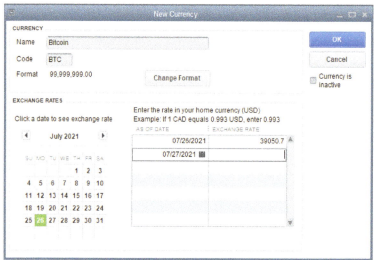

## What is an exchange rate?

As the Currency list describes it in QuickBooks Desktop, the *exchange rate* is the number of home currency units it takes to get 1 foreign currency unit. QuickBooks uses exchange rates to show how much a foreign currency transaction is in your home currency value. QuickBooks also uses exchange rates for your reports.

In the example below, the US Dollar is the home currency. It takes .738715 USD to equal the value of 1 Australian dollar as of the latest date tracked for this currency, which is July 26, 2021.

It takes .797474 USD to equal the value of 1 Canadian dollar as of the latest date. Remember: it's how many units of the home currency you need to equal one unit of the foreign currency.

Here are some rules to remember:

When the exchange rate is *less* than 1, that means that the *foreign currency is worth less* than the home currency. It also means that when you *convert from the **home** currency*, you'll land up with *more units of the foreign currency*. When you *convert from the **foreign** currency*, you'll land up with *fewer units of the home currency*.

Conversely…

When the exchange rate is *more* than 1, that means that the *foreign currency is worth more* than the home currency. It also means that when you *convert from the **home** currency*, you'll land up with *fewer units of the foreign currency*. When you *convert from the **foreign** currency*, you'll land up with *more units of the home currency*.

Here is a handy chart to help you remember the logic of exchange rates and currencies:

| EXCHANGE RATE | CONVERTING HOME TO FOREIGN | CONVERTING FOREIGN TO HOME |
|---|---|---|
| < 1 | More Foreign Units | Fewer Home Units |
| > 1 | Fewer Foreign Units | More Home Units |

If we were looking at a Currency list with the Australian dollar as the home currency, the rate for the US dollar would be the reciprocal of .738715, or 1/.738715, which is 1.3537. That means $1.3537 AUD equals 1 USD.

If we were looking at a Currency list with the Canadian dollar as the home currency, the rate for the US dollar would be the reciprocal of .797474, or 1/.797474, which is 1.25396. That means $1.25396 CAD equals 1 USD.

For those math folks, think of it this way: If you take the number of foreign currency units in a transfer and divide it by the number of home currency units from that transfer, and take that fraction and multiply it by the exchange rate, the product is 1.

Let's take an easy example.

In the case of a foreign currency vs. the home currency, where the exchange rate is .8, that means that the foreign currency is worth .8 of the home currency. Therefore, a transfer of 125 FC units is required to get a home currency value of 100 HC units. Therefore, a transfer of F125/HC100 x the exchange rate of .8:

$$1.25 \times .8 = 1$$

It makes sense, then, that the home currency appears on your Currency list with an exchange rate of 1 or "par." There is no way to edit this exchange rate for the home currency.

Note that QuickBooks Desktop allows for only six decimal places in an exchange rate field. That's why the reciprocal of .797474 for the Canadian dollar exchange rate, which is 1.2539593767, would appear as 1.25396. That is also why the exchange rate for Bitcoin, which is 39,050.70, appears as 39,050.7: there are only six digits allowed in the exchange rate.

| CURRENCY (1 UNIT) | CODE | EXCHANGE RATE | AS OF DATE |
|---|---|---|---|
| Australian Dollar | AUD | .738715 | 07/26/2021 |
| Brazilian Real | BRL | .193248 | 07/26/2021 |
| British Pound Sterling | GBP | 1.38296 | 07/26/2021 |
| Canadian Dollar | CAD | .797474 | 07/26/2021 |
| Chinese Yuan Renminbi | CNY | .154254 | 07/26/2021 |
| Euro | EUR | 1.18105 | 07/26/2021 |
| Japanese Yen | JPY | .009067 | 07/26/2021 |
| Malaysian Ringgit | MYR | .236323 | 07/26/2021 |
| Mexican Peso | MXN | .050002 | 07/26/2021 |
| Singapore Dollar | SGD | .736426 | 07/26/2021 |
| South Korean Won | KRW | .000867 | 07/26/2021 |
| Taiwan Dollar | TWD | .035654 | 07/26/2021 |
| US Dollar | USD | 1 | 07/26/2021 |
| Venezuelan Bolivar | VEB | | |

Currency List

Exchange rate: 1 unit foreign currency = x units home currency
Example: 1 AUD (foreign) = 0.738715 USD (home)

Currency ▼   Activities ▼   Reports ▼   ☐ Include inactive

## Curate the currency list

If you're tracking one or more foreign currencies, you'll be required to curate or maintain the foreign currency list with exchange rates between each foreign currency and your home currency. This means downloading the current exchange rates for every day, or, for missed days in the past, you'll need to enter the exchange rate manually. There is no way to download exchange rates for past dates.

This is important to do right from the very start of your multicurrency usage because QuickBooks picks up what it believes is the exchange rate in force on a foreign transaction's date. If there is no exchange rate entered or downloaded for a particular currency for that date, QuickBooks will pick up the exchange rate that it does have on file for the most recent date *before* the transaction date.

If exchange rates for a currency have never been downloaded or entered for a particular transaction date or prior, QuickBooks will decide that the exchange rate with your country's home currency is 1 or par. And that can cause some inaccurate revenue and expense amounts, understating them, but then the exchange gain or loss account can be wildly overstated.

That's why, as I indicated in a previous lesson, you should go to the Currency list immediately after turning on Multicurrency, choose the currencies you want to see, and download the latest exchange rates. If you need exchange rates for any date before you first downloaded the latest exchange rates, you must enter those prior rates manually. We'll do that together.

## Download latest exchange rates

Select **Lists > Currency List**. Make sure that you have all the currencies you want to see. If you don't see all the currencies you want, at the bottom of the list, select the checkbox next to **Include inactive**. Then click on the **X** next to any inactive currencies you want to make active.

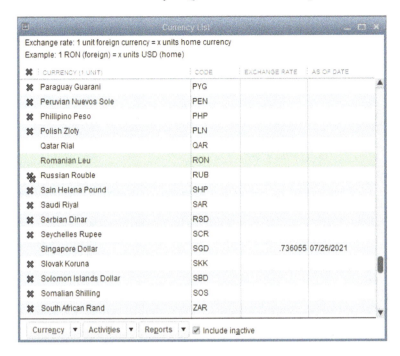

Then click on **Activities > Download Latest Exchange Rates**.

QB updates exchange rates for active currencies only. You'll get a confirmation message, in which you click **OK**.

Then *uncheck* the box next to **Include inactive** to hide all the other currencies you don't want to see.

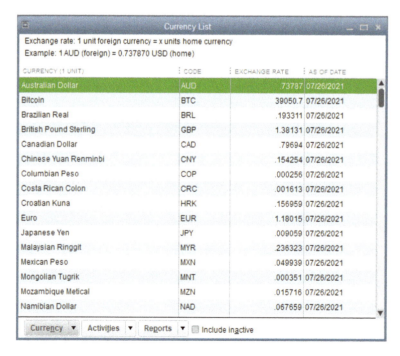

There are some lesser-known currencies that do not have their exchange rates updated by QuickBooks, including the Venezuelan Bolivar and the Estonian Kroon. For those currencies, we have to enter the exchange rates for various dates, including today's date, manually.

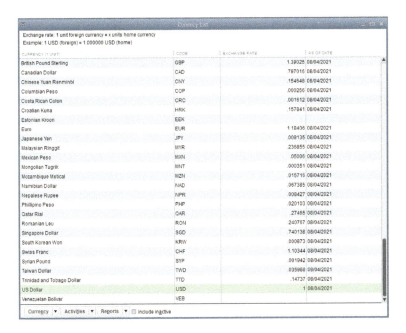

## Manually enter previous exchange rates

Maybe you need to enter exchange rates for various dates for currencies that QuickBooks Desktop doesn't organically have on its Currency list (think of Bitcoin and Parmigiano-Reggiano cheese). Or, suppose we want to enter the exchange rate for some previous dates (or even a future date) for a currency that is on the list. Let's pick the Euro: double-click on the **Euro** in the Currency list:

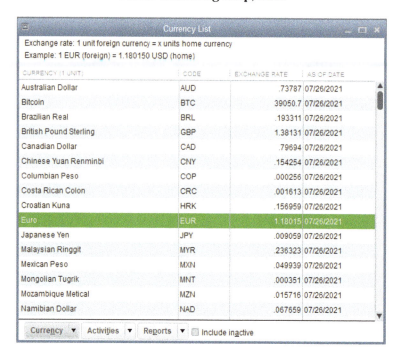

Click on an empty row in the list to add a new date:

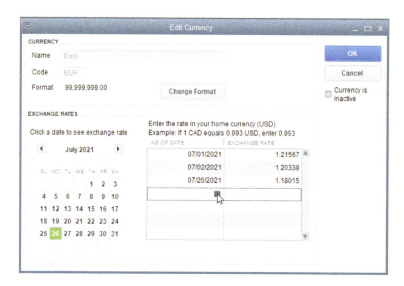

Click on the calendar or enter the date for which you want to add an exchange rate:

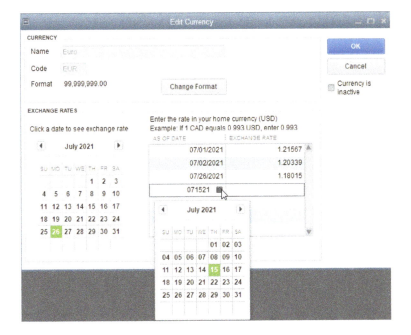

Select **Tab** or mouse click to the exchange rate field. Enter the **exchange rate** for that date.

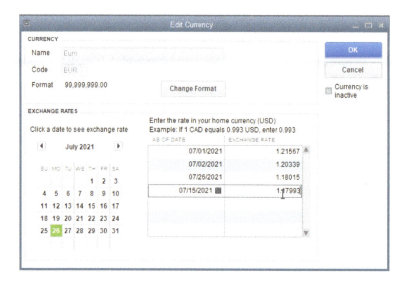

Keep going to the next row to enter more dates and their exchange rates. Select **OK** when you are done. You'll then see the exchange rates for this currency in chronological order.

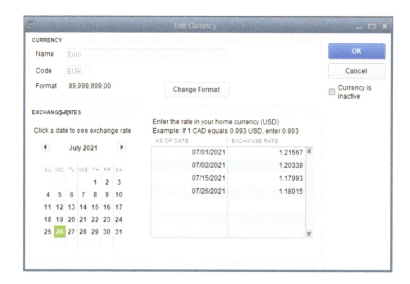

Currency by currency, enter all exchange rates for past dates. You can also double-click on a previously-entered date's row to edit the exchange rate. You can enter exchange rates for future dates, but in most situations you'll keep downloading the latest exchange rates as part of your tasks on each workday.

Some people forget to update the latest exchange rates after they initially do it. So there might be an exchange rate for a currency for, say, January 1 of this year. Let's say the exchange rate is 1.25. Then they forgot to update the exchange rates, either manually or by downloading, as time went on. So every transaction after January 1 using this currency has the default exchange rate of 1.25, even though the rates have changed dramatically over time, say down to .8. The 1.25 exchange rate will populate any transaction using this foreign currency, regardless of date, as long as it is after the initial January 1 rate. Yes, you can edit the exchange rate on individual transactions, but people often forget that the exchange rate field is there. The financials can get really messed up if the exchange rates are not populating properly.

So curate your Currency list! Keep your active currencies' exchange rates updated, either every day by downloading the latest exchange rate or by entering them manually. This is crucial to using QuickBooks Desktop's Multicurrency function properly. Take note, though: you do not have to curate exchange rates in QuickBooks Online.

# Module 2: Foreign Currency Transactions and Exchange Gains and Losses

# Chapter 10
# Sales in Foreign Currency - Workflow and Foreign Exchange Gains/Losses

[Note that we are using very simple exchange rates in these examples, with only one or two digits after the decimal place. Live exchange rates will have more digits.]

Now that Multicurrency has been enabled, you can do so much with foreign currencies in QuickBooks Desktop!

## Foreign invoice

Let's create an invoice in euros to a new customer. The customer doesn't exist yet, so we'll do a Quick Add of the foreign name right on the invoice:

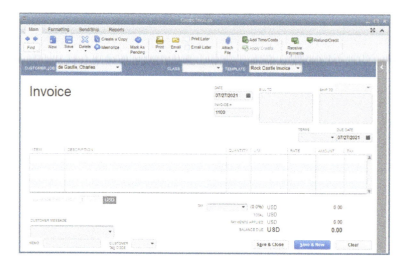

As soon as we hit the TAB key to get to the next field, Quick-Books tells us that this name does not exist: we see the *Customer:Job Not Found* window. We have the option to do a full setup or a Quick Add, but in both cases, we can assign a currency (if we don't assign a currency, QuickBooks will default to the home currency).

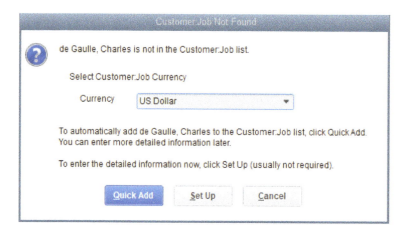

If we choose the **Set up** option, as if we have more contact details for this new customer, we can choose the currency in the **Payment Settings** tab.

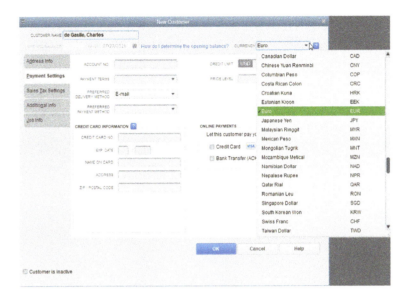

If we cancel out of this and choose the **Quick Add** option, we can select the currency for this customer directly on the *Customer:Job Not Found* window.

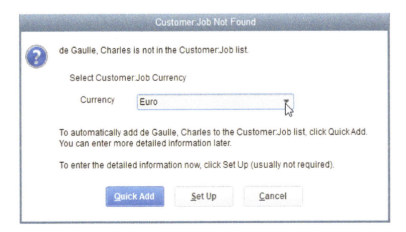

Note that I can go back into the customer and change the currency as long as this customer has not been used in any transactions. Once it has, the currency field is greyed out and can't be changed unless the transactions are deleted.

Also note that the first time you begin to create an invoice or credit memo is launched in a new currency, QuickBooks Desktop creates an Accounts Receivable account for that currency:

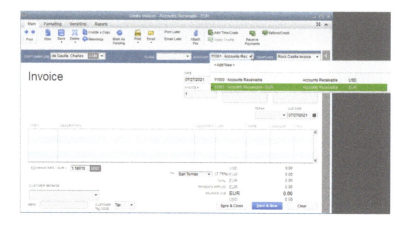

When you choose a customer on an invoice or credit memo, QuickBooks automatically selects an Accounts Receivable account for that customer's currency.

And, as with other situations in QuickBooks Desktop, you can create multiple Accounts Receivable accounts on the Chart of Accounts for any currency. Just go into the Chart of Accounts and create a new account of the type Accounts Receivable and the currency of your choice.

Let's change the date of the invoice to the beginning of the calendar year. It so happens that in this QuickBooks company, we did not create an exchange rate for January 1 of this year or earlier, so it's picking up an exchange rate of 1 with the euro.

We can click **OK** and get out of the invoice to go to the Currency List and assign an exchange rate we pick up from another source, such as xe.com, to January 1 of this year. Or, to make things easier, we can just overwrite the pre-populated exchange rate on the invoice with what we know to be the correct exchange rate on that date.

Let's pretend we looked up the exchange rate for the euro on January 1 and found that it's 1.2, which means that a euro is worth $1.20 in our home currency. We've overwritten the exchange rate right on the invoice. Now let's populate all the fields using euros on the invoice:

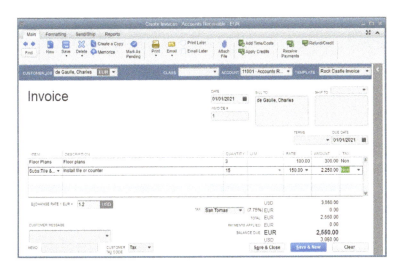

When the customer receives the invoice, they see only the foreign amounts and totals, although we see those as well as the amounts in the foreign currency at the exchange rate we used in the onscreen invoice. We can see that the foreign total is 2,550 euro while the home currency amount is $3,060.

Now let's click on **Save** (or **Save & Close** or **Save & New**).

There are two consequences to what we just did.

First, if we open the Currency List and double click on **Euro**, we can see that the exchange rate for January 1 is 1.2. QuickBooks saved it for us so we don't have to overwrite the exchange rate for this currency on other transactions for that date or later unless we want to do so.

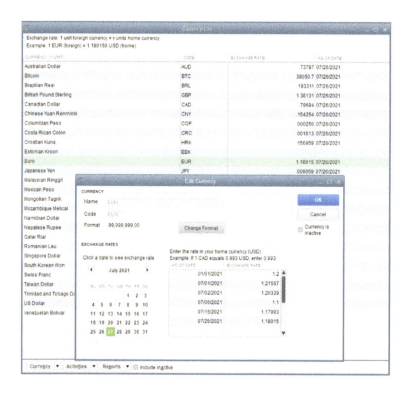

Secondly, if we look at the debits and credits behind the scenes for this invoice (**Ctrl+Y** or **Reports > Transaction Journal** in the ribbon header), we can see the amounts in the home currency only. If we want to see the amounts in the original foreign currency, we can click on **Customize Report** and then **Display** to check the column for **Foreign Amount**. Click **OK**.

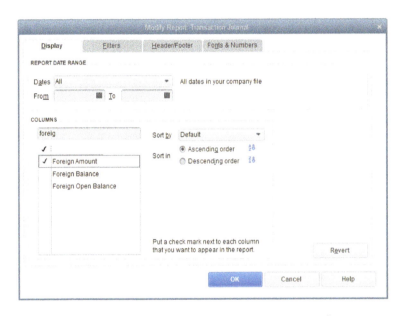

The Transaction Journal now displays a column for foreign amount. Note that there is no choice of "foreign debit" and "foreign credit" in QuickBooks Desktop. They are, however, available in QuickBooks Online.

If we wanted to, we could also display columns for the currency and the exchange rate. This will come in very handy later on.

If we run a Balance Sheet as of January 1, we'll see the home currency amount in the Accounts Receivable - EUR account. Summary reports such as the Balance Sheet and the Profit and Loss display totals and balances in the home currency only. But we can get detailed reports on any foreign account on the Balance Sheet, and those reports can display foreign amounts. Here, I'm double-clicking on the amount for the Accounts Receivable - EUR account, and I can customize it for the date range and to add the Foreign Amount.

We can also run an Accounts Receivable report such as the Open Invoices report. We can filter it for only a particular accounts receivable account such as Accounts Receivable - EUR. Like any QuickBooks report that has filters, it's a good practice to re-title the report so people know exactly what they're looking at.

Further, we can customize the report to display the **Foreign Open Balance** instead of the Open Balance in the home currency..

## Foreign receive payment

Let's pretend the customer paid the invoice on February 15. We start the Receive Payment process. As soon as we enter or select the euro customer in the *Received From* field and select **TAB** to get to the next one, the A/R account changes automatically to the euro one and the payment amount field changes from the home currency to euro. Let's assume they're paying the entire invoice:

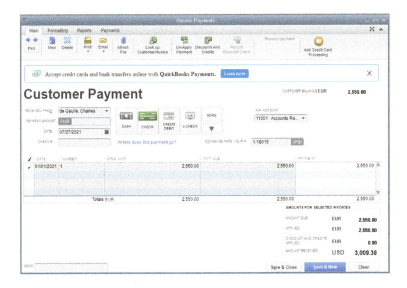

We see an Exchange Rates window pop up, telling us that by changing the date on this transaction, there should be a new exchange rate appearing. Click **OK**:

Now, in this company, we have not updated any exchange rates for the euro earlier in the year, except for accepting the 1.2 rate for January 1. So QuickBooks is offering the same 1.2 exchange rate at February 15, because there are no other populated exchange rates on or before February 15 on the Currency List for the euro.

We consult our exchange rates online and find that the rate on February 15 is 1.45 so let's overwrite the exchange rate on this entry:

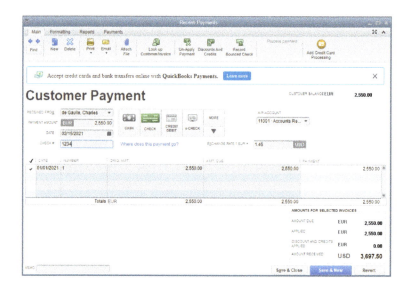

Now notice that the 2,550 euro payment is worth $3,697.50 at that new rate of exchange. Let's choose **Save & New**. Now we're in an empty Receive Payment window. We want to go back to the one we just saved, so let's click on the **Previous arrow**. Let's hit **Control+Y** or look at the Transaction Journal:

Also, let's customize the report to display the exchange rate, currency, and foreign amounts:

Notice the account called *Exchange Gain or Loss*. This is an *Other Expense* type of account that QuickBooks created automatically as soon as it automatically posted a gain or loss on foreign exchange.

That's right....QuickBooks automatically calculated and posted a gain in this case on foreign exchange. It's a gain and so it's a credit. Had it been a loss, it would have been a debit. Here's what QuickBooks calculated:

On January 1, there was an invoice for 2,550 euro. At that time, the home currency equivalent due to the 1.2 exchange rate was

$3,060.00. That means that at the time of invoicing, we expected to receive the foreign equivalent of our home currency $3,060.00.

But then, by the time the invoice was paid on February 15, the exchange rate changed - this time, an increase, to 1.45. So the same 2,550 euro invoice was worth, at the time of payment, $3,697.50 in our home currency, or $637.50 more than we expected at the time of invoicing.

So QuickBooks posted a *foreign exchange gain* of $637.50 automatically on this payment transaction.

As far as the customer is concerned, they're paid in full and they don't care about our home currency. *They care only about their payable in euros.* So the full amount of the original invoice paid (in euros and in dollars, the home currency) is applied against the euro accounts receivable. Any difference in the home currency value at the time of payment is applied to exchange gain or loss.

So on receivables, when the exchange rate goes up on the foreign currency, we benefit from a gain on foreign exchange. If the exchange rates drops on the foreign currency, we suffer a loss on foreign exchange.

Let's take a look at the Currency List again: now there is a rate of 1.45 for the euro on February 15. Ideally, of course, we would have updated the currency's exchange rates for many dates, not those that are a month and a half apart.

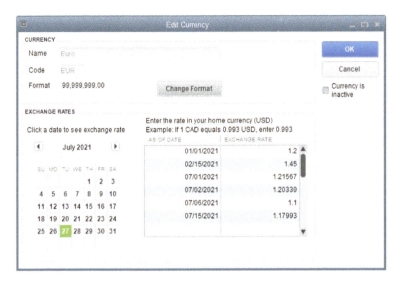

That was Step 1 of getting our money. In this company file, the default is to put monies received into Undeposited Funds (if we had chosen to put the money from the Receive Payment transaction directly into a bank account, there would be no further step). So there's a Step 2 to put this money into the bank account. We could receive it into our home currency checking ("chequing" for us Canadians) account or we could put it into a euro-denominated bank account that we would create.

Warning: if you receive a payment and don't apply it to one or more foreign invoices, just leaving the payment unapplied, no exchange gain or loss will be calculated.

## Depositing into the bank account - Domestic (home currency) account

Let's put it into our domestic (i.e. home currency) bank account on February 20. We select that we want to make a bank deposit, and we need to select from the drop-down that we want to view payments in the euro currency:

## Esther Friedberg Karp, MBA

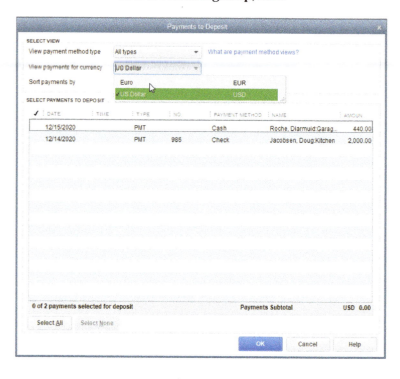

## Multicurrency in QuickBooks® Desktop

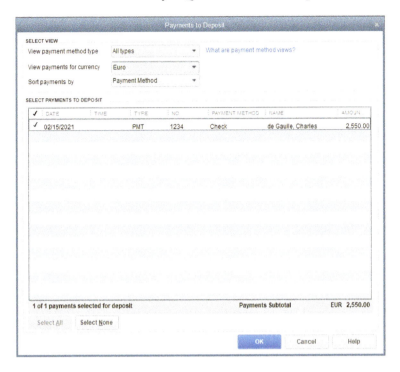

We check the box next to the payment from Charles de Gaulle and select **OK**. We indicate that the deposit is going into the Checking account (a home currency account). We change the date to February 20. Had we updated the exchange rate for the euro in the Currency List for February 20, it would appear by default in the exchange rate field. But we're only getting the exchange rate we updated for February 15, being the 1.45.

So for sure we want to update the exchange rate for February 20 on the deposit transaction, but this time we need to refer to another source for the rate. This time, we need to use the bank's exchange rate because they're going to give us a specific amount in dollars for the euro deposit. In all likelihood, the bank will give us a rate that is not as good as we could get elsewhere, because, let's face it: banks always take their piece to make money.

Let's assume that the bank says that the euro is worth only 1.3 on February 20 (in reality, they would give us a rate that had several decimals after the point):

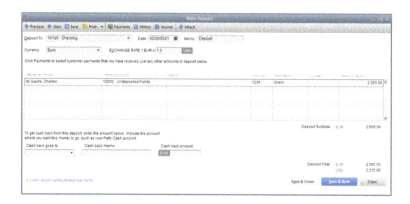

We hit **Save & New** and then click on **Previous**. Let's look at the Transaction Journal:

And let's customize this report by adding the currency, exchange rate, and foreign amount columns:

This time, there is a debit amount in the Exchange Gain or Loss figure row. That's a loss. That's because since the last time the amount was valued in the home currency, on February 15 at 1.45 ($3,697.50), the exchange rate for the euro fell. Therefore, despite expecting $3,697.50 on February 15, we incurred a loss of $382.50 and only $3,315 showed up in our bank account on February 20.

Also, the Currency List now shows 1.3 as the exchange rate for the euro on February 20:

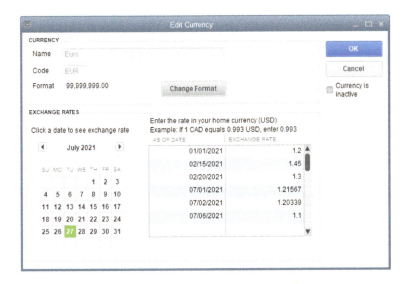

Let's take a look at the Profit & Loss for the period from February 15th through the 20th. Let's display the columns by day.

Notice that on February 15, we had a gain (a negative expense) of $637.50 on foreign exchange for the Receive Payment transaction, Step 1. On February 20, we had a loss (a positive expense) of $382.50 on foreign exchange for the Deposit transaction, Step 2. The total gain on foreign exchange for those six days is $255 (a negative expense), which is the sum of these two steps.

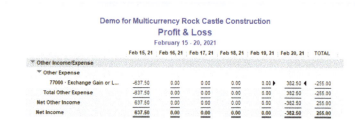

## Depositing into the bank account - foreign currency account

If we had deposited the funds directly into a euro-denominated bank account instead of a home currency one, here's what would happen:

I'm editing the Make Deposit transaction to deposit the funds from this received payment into a new account, the Euro Bank Account. I'm going to set it up on the spot.

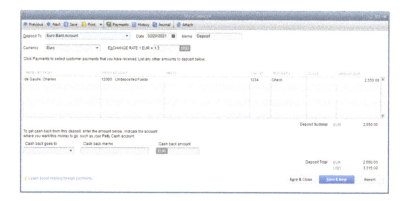

A bank account is one of the four account types in QuickBooks Desktop to which we can assign a currency (the others are credit cards, accounts receivable, and accounts payable).

We are assigning the euro to this bank account. If we'd made a mistake in assigning the currency, we could change the currency as long as we didn't create any transactions involving this account.

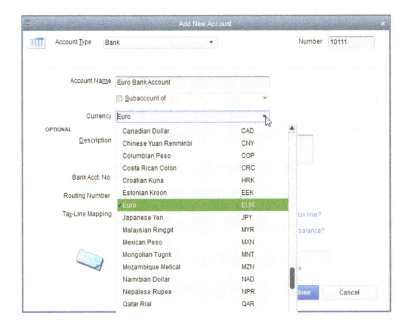

Let's assume that the euro exchange rate we picked up from xe.com for February 20 was 1.37. We can overwrite the pre-populated exchange rate in this transaction if 1.37 is not set up as the rate for this date on the Currency List. In our case, we already have 1.3 in the Currency List for this date, so we'll over-write it:

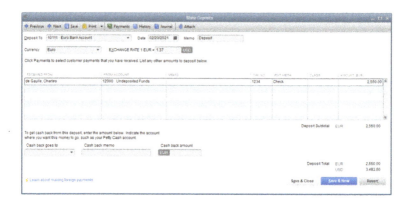

We're changing the exchange rate to 1.37 from the 1.3 that is in the Currency List. Let's choose **Save & New** ...and we get this message that we are attempting to change the previously-popu-lated exchange rate for February 20. QuickBooks wants to know if we want the new rate, 1.37, to overwrite the old one of 1.3 on the Currency List for the Euro. If we say **Yes**, it will do so and this will be the default euro rate on future transactions for this date. If we say **No**, it will keep the 1.3 on the Currency List but use the 1.37 for this transaction only. (Most of the time, we'll select **No** if the pre-existing exchange rate is more realistic for future transactions with this date.) Let's choose **Yes**.

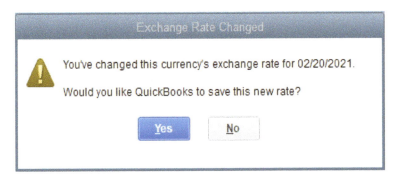

Now let's select **Previous**. Let's look at **Control+Y**. And let's add the columns for the currency, exchange rate, and foreign amount:

Now this deposit transaction yields a loss on foreign exchange of $204. That's because since the last time the amount was valued in the home currency, on February 15 at 1.45 ($3,697.50), the exchange rate for the euro fell. Therefore, despite expecting $3,697.50 on February 15, we incurred a loss of $204 and only the equivalent of $3,493.50 showed up in our euro bank account on February 20.

The Profit & Loss for the six days now shows a total gain on foreign exchange of $433.50:

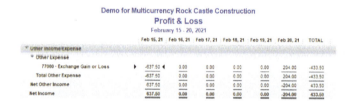

Demo for Multicurrency Rock Castle Construction
**Profit & Loss**
February 15 - 20, 2021

| | Feb 15, 21 | Feb 16, 21 | Feb 17, 21 | Feb 18, 21 | Feb 19, 21 | Feb 20, 21 | TOTAL |
|---|---|---|---|---|---|---|---|
| **Other Income/Expense** | | | | | | | |
| **Other Expense** | | | | | | | |
| 77000 · Exchange Gain or Loss | ▶ -637.50 ◄ | 0.00 | 0.00 | 0.00 | 0.00 | 204.00 | -433.50 |
| **Total Other Expense** | -637.50 | 0.00 | 0.00 | 0.00 | 0.00 | 204.00 | -433.50 |
| **Net Other Income** | 637.50 | 0.00 | 0.00 | 0.00 | 0.00 | -204.00 | 433.50 |
| **Net Income** | 637.50 | 0.00 | 0.00 | 0.00 | 0.00 | -204.00 | 433.50 |

Notice that on February 15, we had a gain (a negative expense) of $637.50 on foreign exchange for the Receive Payment transaction, Step 1. On February 20, we had a loss (a positive expense) of $204 on foreign exchange for the Deposit transaction, Step 2. The total gain on foreign exchange for those six days is $433.50 (a negative expense), which is the sum of these two steps.

## Foreign bank account register

To display the euro bank account register, we double-click on the account in the Chart of Accounts. We see this warning about Foreign Currency Registers:

Foreign Currency Registers ✕

ⓘ Transactions in foreign currency registers can't be edited directly in the register.

Use the Edit Transaction button in the register to make changes.

☐ Do not display this message in the future

**OK**

We click **OK.**

Now the foreign bank account register displays. As it is denominated in foreign currency, we see only the foreign amounts and balances in this register:

If we had right-clicked on the account in the Chart of Accounts and chosen to display the QuickReport, we would see only the home currency values:

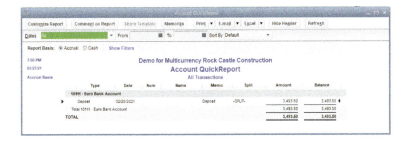

To see the foreign amounts and balances, we have to customize this report to add columns for the Foreign Amount and Foreign Balance columns. We could also add columns for the exchange rate (and move columns around) if we wanted:

## Foreign accounts receivable register

Similar to the foreign bank account, we can display the foreign accounts receivable register, and it displays only foreign amounts and balances:

Showing a QuickReport on the foreign accounts receivable, and adding extra columns and moving them around, gives us this information:

We have now covered how QuickBooks automatically calculates and records gains and losses on foreign exchange based on transactions in a sales workflow.

## Selling on the spot: sales receipts

If we sold to a foreign customer using a sales receipt rather than an invoice, and if the money went directly into a bank account, there would be no gain or loss on foreign exchange. Quick-Books would just record the foreign and home currency values on that sales transaction.

If the sales receipt funds went into Undeposited Funds, then there would be a second step, the Make Deposits transaction, of QuickBooks calculating and automatically recording the gain or loss on foreign exchange.

## The risk of invoicing in another currency

So when invoicing a foreign customer in their currency, be aware that there's a risk if they don't pay on the spot. If the foreign currency's exchange rate drops (i.e., it weakens) by the time they pay, and especially if that money has to be converted into your home currency immediately, we'll receive less than we expected and incur a loss. If the foreign currency's exchange rate rises (i.e., it strengthens) by the time they pay, no worries - you're enjoying a gain!

And regardless of whether the exchange rate weakens or strengthens, QuickBooks Desktop will automatically calculate the gain or loss and record it for you.

## Foreign invoice from an estimate or sales order

We can issue estimates or sales orders for a foreign customer and turn them into foreign invoices. There is no gain or loss on foreign exchange because estimates and sales orders are non-posting transactions, so nothing hits the general ledger until an invoice is created.

## Foreign prices

In this example, we had an invoice with no default selling prices in which we entered the foreign price in euros. Had there been a saved selling price for these items, we would have had to over-write them to reflect the agreed-upon euro selling price. But there is a great workaround and we will cover how to maintain static foreign price lists for items in sales transactions later in this book.

# Chapter 11
# Purchases in Foreign Currency - Workflow and Foreign Exchange Gains/Losses

[Note that we are using very simple exchange rates in these examples, with only one or two digits after the decimal place. Live exchange rates will have more digits.]

Gains or losses on foreign exchange due to exchange rate swings also impact foreign purchase transactions...but the effect is the opposite to what happens on sales transactions.

## Foreign bill

Let's create a bill in Australian dollars from a new vendor. The Aussie vendor doesn't exist yet, so we'll do a Quick Add of the foreign name right on the bill:

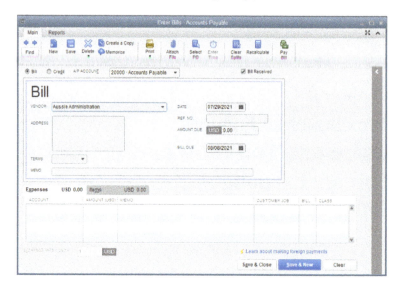

As soon as we hit the TAB key to get to the next field, Quick-Books tells us that this name does not exist: we see the *Vendor Not Found* window. We have the option to do a full setup or a Quick Add, but in both cases, we can assign a currency (if we don't assign a currency, QuickBooks will default to the home currency).

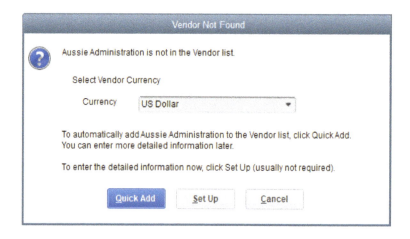

If we choose the **Set up** option, as if we have more contact details for this new vendor, we can choose the currency in the **Payment Settings** tab.

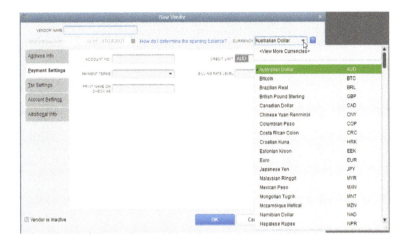

If we cancel out of this and choose the **Quick Add** option, we can select the currency for this customer directly on the *Vendor Not Found* window.

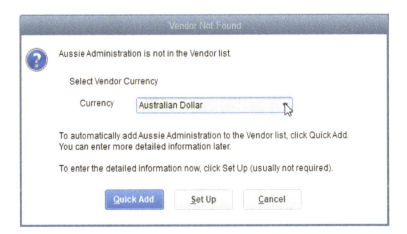

Note that I can go back into the vendor and change the currency as long as this vendor has not been used in any transactions.

Once it has, the currency field is greyed out and can't be changed unless the transactions are deleted.

Also note that the first time you begin to create a bill or bill credit is launched in a new currency, QuickBooks Desktop creates an Accounts Payable account for that currency:

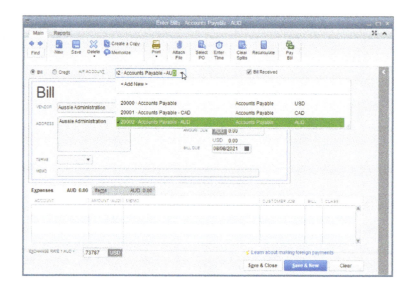

When you choose a supplier on a bill or bill credit, QuickBooks automatically selects an Accounts Payable account for that supplier's currency.

And, as with other situations in QuickBooks Desktop, you can create multiple Accounts Payable accounts on the Chart of Accounts for any currency. Just go into the Chart of Accounts and create a new account of the type Accounts Payable and the currency of your choice.

Let's change the date of the bill to the beginning of the calendar year. It so happens that in this QuickBooks company, we did not create an exchange rate for January 1 of this year or earlier, so it's picking up an exchange rate of 1 with the Aussie dollar.

We can click **OK** and get out of the bill to go to the Currency List and assign an exchange rate we picked up from another source, such as xe.com, to January 1 of this year for this currency. Or, to make things easier, we can just overwrite the pre-populated exchange rate on the invoice with what we know to be the correct exchange rate on that date.

Let's pretend we looked up the exchange rate for the Aussie dollar on January 1 and found that it was .75, which means that an Australian dollar was worth 75 cents in our home currency. We've overwritten the exchange rate for the Aussie dollar right on the bill. Now let's populate all the fields using Australian dollars on the bill:

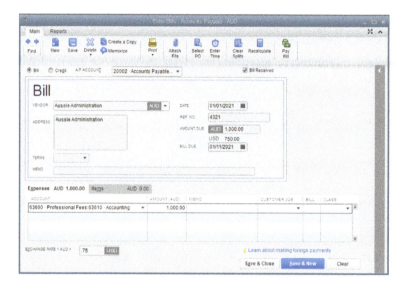

We see both the foreign total ($1,000 AUD) and the home currency ($750 USD) totals on the onscreen bill, based on the exchange rate for that date. The vendor does not receive a copy of this bill, so this information is solely for the benefit of your company staff.

Now let's click on **Save** (or **Save & Close** or **Save & New**).

There are two consequences to what we just did.

First, if we open the Currency List and double click on **Australian Dollar**, we can see that the exchange rate for January 1 is .75. QuickBooks saved it for us so we don't have to overwrite the exchange rate for this currency on other transactions for that date or later unless we want to do so.

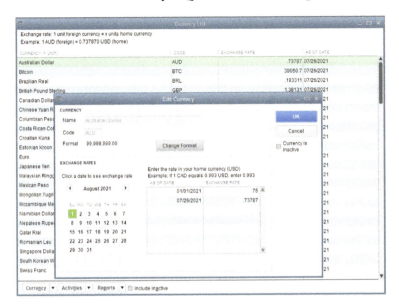

Secondly, if we look at the debits and credits behind the scenes for this invoice (**Ctrl+Y** or **Reports > Transaction Journal** in the ribbon header), we can see the amounts in the home currency only. If we want to see the amounts in the original foreign currency, we can click on **Customize Report** and then **Display** to check the column for **Currency**, **Exchange Rate**, **Foreign Amount**. Click **OK**.

If we run a Balance Sheet as of January 1, we'll see the home currency amount in the Accounts Payable - AUD account. Remember: summary reports such as the Balance Sheet and the Profit and Loss display totals and balances in the home currency only. But we can get detailed reports such as a Transactions by Account on any foreign account on the Balance Sheet, and those reports can display foreign amounts. Here, I'm double-clicking on the amount for the Accounts Payable - AUD account, and I can customize it for the date range and to add the Foreign Amount.

We can also run an Accounts Payable report such as the Unpaid Bills Detail report. We can filter it for only a particular accounts receivable account such as Accounts Payable - AUD. Like any QuickBooks report that has filters, it's a good practice to re-title the report so people know exactly what they're looking at.

Further, we can customize the report to display the **Foreign Open Balance** instead of the Open Balance in the home currency..

## Foreign pay bills

Let's pretend we paid the bill in full on February 28. We start the Pay Bills process. This time, we have to specify which Accounts Payable account we're addressing. We choose the **Accounts Payable - AUD** account. Let's pretend we're paying it out of our home currency Checking account. (This example would also work well if we were paying it out of a home currency credit card account.) The bank always charges more on foreign exchange to add to its bottom line. We're "buying" Australian Dollars to pay this vendor, so the bank will make

Australian dollars more expensive than the default exchange rate. Let's overwrite the exchange rate to .8.

Now look at what happens on this Pay Bills screen: we're paying the $1,000 AUD in full, and that's all the vendor cares about. He or she doesn't know or care about what it's worth to us in our home currency. But at the bank's overpriced .8 Australian exchange rate, that Australian amount is now worth $800 in our home currency, rather than the $750 equivalent we thought we'd pay when the bill was issued.

We can predict, then, that we will suffer a *loss* on foreign exchange as a result of this payment:

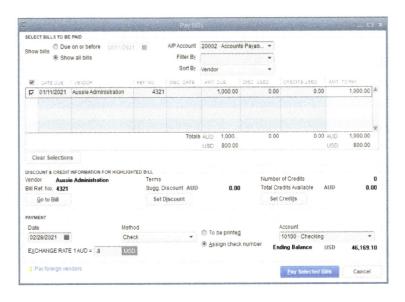

Let's choose **Pay Selected Bills**, then assign a check number and then select **Done**.

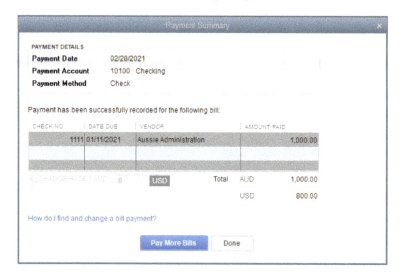

Now let's go into the Vendor Center to find that vendor and its transactions. Specifically, we're looking for the Bill Payment transaction dated February 28. We open it and hit **Control+Y** or look at the Transaction Journal:

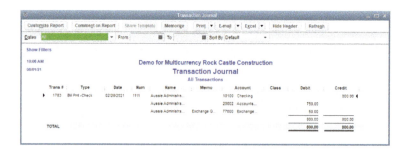

Now let's customize this report to add the **Currency**, **Exchange Rate**, and the **Foreign Amount**:

Sure enough, the Exchange Gain or Loss account, an Other Expense account, indicates a loss because it has a debit amount on this transaction. So again, QuickBooks automatically calculated and posted the effect on the Exchange Gain or Loss account, and this time it was a loss. It's the opposite of what happened when the foreign currency strengthened when we had a foreign invoices outstanding.

So on payables, when the exchange rate goes up on the foreign currency, we suffer a loss on foreign exchange. If the exchange rates drops on the foreign currency, we enjoy a gain on foreign exchange.

Warning: if you pay one or more foreign bills and then un-apply the payment to the bills, or if you write a foreign check to a Vendor and post it to that currency's Accounts Payable, both just leaving the payment unapplied, no exchange gain or loss will be calculated.

Let's take a look at the Currency List again: now there is a rate of .8 for the Australian dollar on February 28. Ideally, of course, we would have updated the currency's exchange rates for many dates, not those that are two months apart.

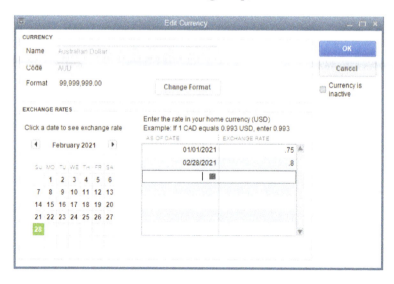

If we had paid the bill out of an Australian dollar-denominated account, such as a bank or credit card account, we would still have to populate the exchange rate field with a rate for that date, but we'd be able to find default rates from xe.com and other sources, rather than the bank overcharging for foreign exchange.

And we'd see the foreign amounts hitting the foreign bank or credit card register. We'd see the home currency values hitting those accounts if we ran a QuickReport on those accounts.

Let's take a look at the Australian dollar Accounts Payable register. We see the amounts in the foreign currency only.

If we run a QuickReport on that account, we see only home currency amounts:

But of course we can customize that report to show the foreign information, including, if we like the Foreign Open Balance:

The Profit & Loss report for February 28 indicates a loss on foreign exchange of $50.

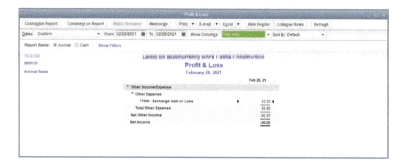

# Buying on the spot: checks and credit card charges

If we bought from a foreign vendor using a check or credit card charge rather than a bill, and if the money came directly out of a bank or credit card account, there would be no gain or loss on foreign exchange. QuickBooks would just record the foreign and home currency values on that purchase transaction.

# The risk of buying in another currency

So when a foreign vendor invoices us in their currency, be aware that there's a risk if we don't pay on the spot. If the foreign currency's exchange rate drops (i.e., it weakens) by the time we have to pay, we'll pay less than we expected and enjoy a gain. If the foreign currency's exchange rate rises (i.e., it strengthens) by the time we pay, we incur a loss.

And regardless of whether the exchange rate weakens or strengthens, QuickBooks Desktop will automatically calculate the gain or loss and record it for you.

# Foreign bill from a purchase order

We can record and issue purchase orders to a foreign vendor and turn them into foreign bills. There is no gain or loss on foreign exchange because purchase orders are non-posting transactions, so nothing hits the general ledger until a bill is created. We will cover foreign purchase orders later in this book.

## Foreign purchase prices

We will also cover foreign currency item costs later in this book. QuickBooks does not handle foreign currency item costs nearly as well as it does foreign currency selling prices. It's quite disappointing, so we have to perform a manual workaround.

# Chapter 12
# Exchange Gain or Loss Account

After conducting some invoicing and receiving of payments (and perhaps depositing to the bank), as well as bills and pay bills, in foreign currency, let's take a look at the *Exchange Gain or Loss* account, which is a special account created by QuickBooks once it starts calculating foreign exchange gains or losses.

## How is the Exchange Gain or Loss account affected?

As we said earlier, it's an Other Expense account, so debits are losses and credits are gains.

Remember, QuickBooks calculates and records the gain or loss on foreign exchange when completing a receivable workflow (receiving payment, and, if it's a separate transaction, depositing into the bank) as exchange rates fluctuate. It also calculates the gain or loss on foreign exchange when completing a payable workflow (paying a bill) as the exchange rates fluctuate.

Think of invoices and bills as *opening* their respective workflows, and think of receiving payment and depositing to the bank, as well as paying bills, as *closing* their respective workflows. QuickBooks calculates and records gains or losses on foreign exchange when we record the closing transactions of these workflows.

A QuickReport of this account will tell us what we need to know so far.

Let's customize this report to take away the Memo, Split, and Amount columns, and replace them with Debit and Credit as well as Currency columns:

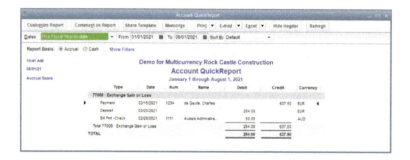

## Get more info by exporting to Excel

This report can be exported to Excel using Advanced options of Auto Outline and Auto Filtering. Then we can use filtering on the Currency column to see how much each currency is benefiting or costing us in terms of gains or losses on foreign exchange.

We can even sort by currency, and create subtotals to give us this information by currency all in one report.

## What transaction types to expect

Because sales-based and purchase-based workflows have their gains or losses on foreign exchange recorded only when these workflows are closed, you can expect three types of transactions in the Exchange Gain or Loss account:

- Payment (i.e. invoice payment)
- Deposit (i.e. to the bank if an invoice is paid or a sales receipt is linked to Undeposited funds)
- Bill Payment (by check or credit card)

We will be discussing one other situation that leads to entries (spoiler alert: it's a special type of general journal entry) in the Gain or Loss on Foreign Exchange account later in this book. And then we will discuss checking for fraud in a QuickBooks company file, so stay tuned for more on this account!

# Chapter 13
# Transfers Between Currencies

As many QuickBooks users know, there are several ways to record transfers between bank and/or credit card accounts. They have a choice of a Transfer Funds transaction, a Check, a Deposit, Credit Card Charge or Credit, and, of course, Journal Entries.

However, in a Multicurrency company, if you want to transfer funds between accounts of different currencies, there is only one choice that will be simple and effective: the Transfer Funds transaction. The other choices can be quite problematic.

## Multicurrency transfers: one account is in the home currency

If you are transferring funds between accounts of two currencies, and one of them is the home currency, this is super easy.

Let's take the example of the US Checking account and the Euro Bank account:

If we want to transfer funds between them, all we need to do is to use the Transfer Funds transaction, choose the **date**, our **from** and **to** accounts, the **currency** of the transfer, and the **exchange rate** mandated by the bank (or credit card company if one of those accounts is a credit card).

In our example, we're moving funds from the US Checking account on August 2 to the Euro account. We have told the bank we want 10,000 Euros to show up in the Euro account.

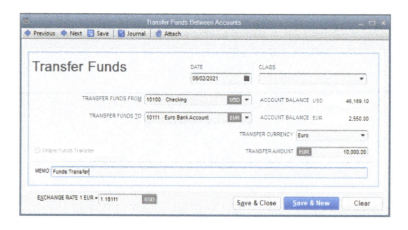

But wait! The exchange rate that pops up is the default rate for August 2 provided by QuickBooks. Surely the bank will want a piece of the action. So the bank will mandate a rate that makes the transfer more expensive to us. Instead of this default rate, the bank charges us something outrageous like an exchange rate of 1.3. So we overwrite the exchange rate and, for good measure, we add the bank's confirmation number to the memo line:

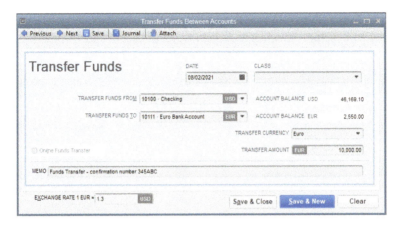

Let's choose **Save** at the top of the transaction. Now let's either click on **Journal** at the top or hit **Control+Y** on the keyboard:

Now let's customize the report to add extra columns for **Currency**, **Exchange Rate**, and **Foreign Amount**:

Let's take a look at the two registers involved in this transaction:

The USD Checking account, the home currency account, shows the $13,000 USD coming out on August 2:

The Euro Bank Account shows the 10,000 Euro going into the account on the same date:

Had we wanted to transfer funds the other way, from the foreign currency to the home currency, that would have been fine as well. We just have to remember to enter the transfer amount in whatever currency is easiest to use, and to be sure to overwrite the exchange rate with the outrageous rate the bank quoted us.

Notice that a multicurrency Transfer Funds transaction does not involve any exchange gains or losses.

## Multicurrency transfers: both accounts are foreign currency

What if we wanted to transfer funds between Foreign Currency A and Foreign Currency B? That's a little more involved. If we create an Australian Chequing account in a US home currency company and we want to transfer 2,000 Euros to it from the Euro account (and the resulting amount in Australian dollars is $3,225.81 AUD):

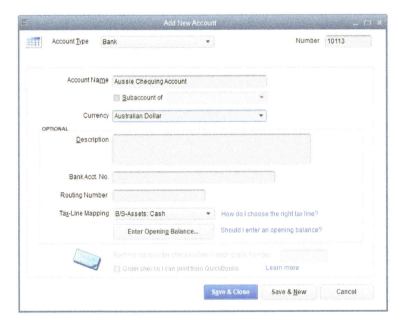

Let's create a Transfer Funds transaction in which both accounts are foreign currency. As soon as we populate the two currencies, we get this warning window:

The reason is that QuickBooks doesn't allow transactions involving two foreign currencies. So we have to chop up the transfer into two. Let's click **OK** and put the transfer aside for a minute.

Here's how we do it.

First, let's create a Clearing Bank account in the home currency for uses like this. Our Clearing bank account balance, when we are finished using it at any given time, will be zero.

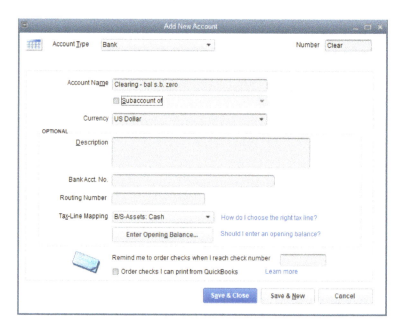

So what we'll do is split the transfer into two: transfer from the Euro to the home currency Clearing account, and transfer from the home currency Clearing account to the Aussie Dollar Chequing.

## Step 1: Transfer from Euro (Foreign Currency A) to the Clearing Account

Here, we transfer funds temporarily to the Clearing Account. We can use whatever reasonable exchange rate pops up. In our case, the 1.3 comes up from the last time. We are transferring 2,000 Euros.

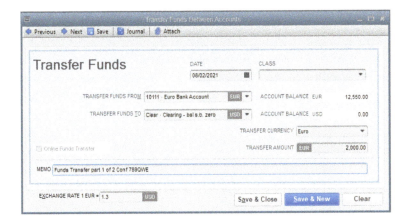

We click **Save & New**. Now look at the Clearing Account to see the home currency balance of $2,600 USD.

## Step 2: Transfer from the Clearing Account to Australian Dollars (Foreign Currency B):

Here, we transfer all the funds related to this transaction out of the Clearing Account. We know that we have to use up the entire $2,600 USD to end up as $3,225.81 AUD. So we can use a physical calculator, or we can use the QuickBooks Desktop Currency Calculator, which is lurking in any multicurrency company file.

## Use the QuickBooks Desktop Currency Calculator

To access the QuickBooks Currency Calculator, select **Company > Manage Currency > Currency Calculator** or select **Control+Alt+C** on your keyboard.

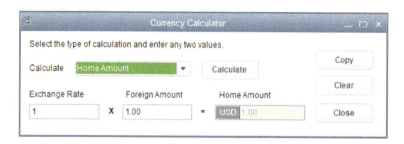

The Currency Calculator allows you to enter two variables and it calculates the third. The variables are:

- Home amount
- Foreign amount
- Exchange rate

We need to calculate the exchange rate that fits a home currency amount of $2,600 USD and a foreign currency amount of $3,225.81 AUD.

We click on the drop-down to calculate the **exchange rate**. We populate the **Foreign Amount** and **Home Amount** fields and click on **Calculate**. The resulting Exchange Rate is .805999:

So let's enter Step 2 for the same date and we even enter the details of the transfer transaction in the Memo line. It's easiest to enter the **Transfer Currency** as USD based on the round amount:

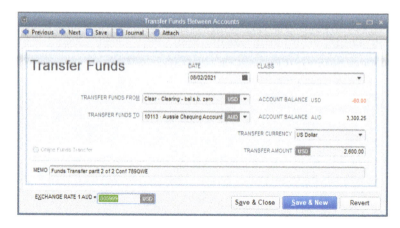

Let's hit **Save** and check the accounts. We could open the register of each bank account but it's faster to look at the balance of each on the Chart of Accounts, because they are displayed in their respective currencies:

The Aussie Chequing Account has a balance of $3,225.81 AUD and the US Clearing Account has a zero balance, which it should always have when we are finished using it for any particular purpose:

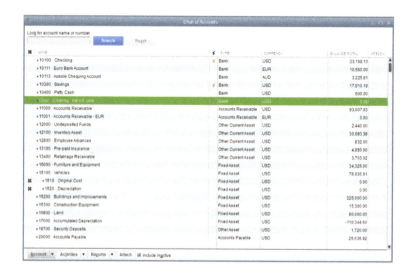

And so all is right with the world...and we know how to transfer funds between currencies.

Also, remember to use the QuickBooks Desktop Currency Calculator in all kinds of situations where you know the values of two of these variables and need to calculate the third:

- Home amount
- Foreign amount
- Exchange rate

Also, remember that in QuickBooks, transferring funds from one currency's account to another does not result in any gain or loss on exchange. The gains or losses are triggered by paying a foreign bill, receiving payment on a foreign invoice, depositing that payment into the bank, or by creating a home currency adjustment.

# Module 3: Foreign Currency Transactions in QuickBooks Desktop - Beyond the Basics

# Chapter 14
# Home Currency Adjustments and the Exchange Gain or Loss Account

We've covered situations in which QuickBooks automatically calculates and records gains and losses on foreign exchange. These situations have to do with closing a sales workflow (receiving payment, depositing to the bank) and closing a purchase workflow (paying a bill).

But there is one more kind of gain or loss on foreign exchange that QuickBooks doesn't record unless we tell it to do so: Home Currency Adjustments. Why do we need to do this?

Let's take a very simple scenario.

### Mattresses stuffed with Klingon cash

Instead of maintaining a foreign currency denominated bank account, imagine that you have stuffed a mattress with foreign cash that belongs to your company. Choose the foreign currency: yen, euros, pesos, ...let's say Klingon darseks just for fun. Just imagine that you stuffed a mattress with 100,000 Klingon darseks on the first day of last year. And you recorded its value in your home currency (at the exchange rate for that day) on your company's balance sheet. Let's say they were worth 120,000 of your home currency's monetary units (e.g. CAD, USD, AUD, Euro, etc.).

Now further imagine that during the course of last year, you didn't touch that Klingon cash. You didn't take out funds to purchase anything for the company, and you didn't add to the funds from sales to customers in that currency either.

So at the end of last year, you still have that mattress stuffed with 100,000 Klingon darseks.

Since exchange rates fluctuate all the time, however, it is very likely that at year-end, those 100,000 darseks are not worth 120,000 of your monetary units anymore. Perhaps they're worth only 105,000 in your currency.

QuickBooks Desktop's automatic calculations of gains and losses on foreign exchange due to sales and purchase transactions that we covered won't cover this situation at all. Foreign balances are worth different amounts depending on the day and the exchange rate. We need to re-value the amount of foreign cash we have in our own home currency at specific milestone dates during the year (whether it's month-end, quarter-end, or year-end...that's up to the individual company).. And that's covering a very simple situation in which no foreign monies left or were added to the mattress.

Therefore, there is the transaction type Home Currency Adjustment, which is exclusive to Multicurrency companies in Quick-Books Desktop. In this situation, we would create a Home Currency Adjustment to re-value the mattress contents so that they appear on the Balance Sheet on the year-end date as 105,000 of your currency, not 120,000 as they did on January 1. The 15,000 unit loss would appear on your Profit & Loss Statement for the year in the Gain or Loss on Foreign Exchange account. The Home Currency Adjustment is not performed for us automatically by QuickBooks; we must launch it manually, specifying the currency and accounts denominated in that currency we want to re-value on a certain date.

Furthermore, if there are transactions affecting the amount of foreign cash in that mattress throughout the year, that only further complicates the need to re-value the balance in our home currency at various milestone dates.

The mattress analogy is for assets, such as bank accounts and accounts receivable in foreign currency.

If you want to extend that analogy to liabilities, such as accounts payable and credit cards in foreign currency, imagine that you are holding on to a mattress stuffed with Klingon darseks for another company. It's not your money, correct? In other words, you owe that company whatever's in the mattress.

As that mattress contains funds that you owe to another entity (the credit card company, or a foreign vendor), due to fluctuating exchange rates, the foreign cash contents of that mattress need to be re-valued at certain milestone dates.

## General ledger account types

Now that we've covered why we need the Home Currency Adjustment, let's return to actual general ledger balances instead of mattresses stuffed with foreign cash we either own or owe to others.

Because QuickBooks Desktop allows for only certain types of accounts on the Balance Sheet to be denominated in foreign currency, only those accounts can be included in a Home Currency Adjustment:

- Bank accounts
- Credit card accounts
- Accounts receivable
- Accounts payable

As far as milestone dates are concerned: most companies perform a Home Currency Adjustment at their fiscal year-end only, but some larger companies have so many foreign currency transactions with such large amounts and balances that they perform the Home Currency Adjustment every month-end.

For each milestone date on which you wish to create a Home Currency Adjustment, you must segregate it into the various foreign currencies in which there are balances.

Let's enter a few more foreign receivables and payables at later dates...say March 31. Let's leave these as unpaid.

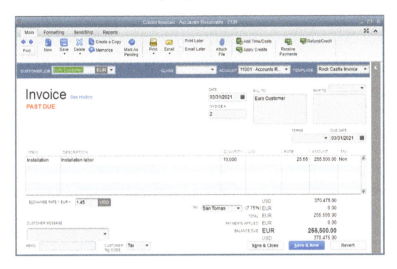

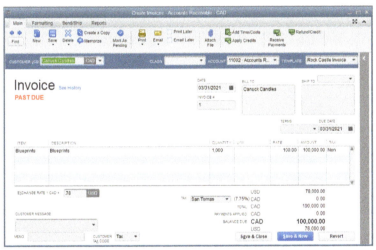

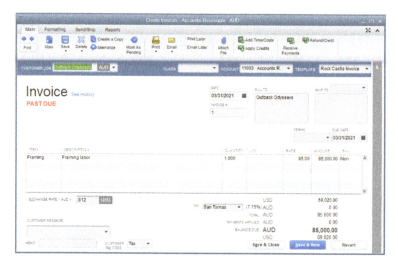

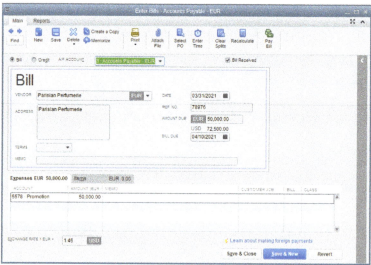

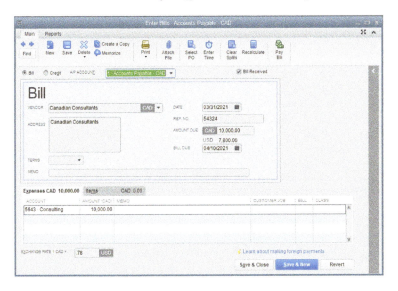

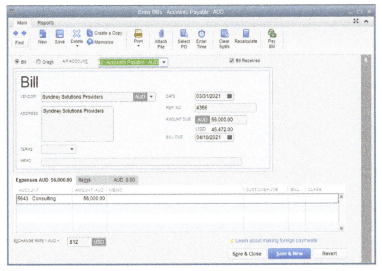

Let's create a Home Currency Adjustment in our company file as of June 30.

The Balance Sheet for that date indicates we have balances in the Euro, CAD, and AUD accounts for Accounts Receivable, and those same Euro, CAD, and AUD accounts for Accounts Payable.

**Demo for Multicurrency Rock Castle Construction**
**Balance Sheet**
As of June 30, 2021

|  | Jun 30, 21 |
|---|---:|
| 10400 · Petty Cash | 500.00 |
| **Total Checking/Savings** | 68,072.79 |
| ▼ **Accounts Receivable** | |
| 11000 · Accounts Receivable | 93,007.93 |
| 11001 · Accounts Receivable - EUR | 370,475.00 |
| 11002 · Accounts Receivable - CAD | 78,000.00 |
| 11003 · Accounts Receivable - AUD | 69,020.00 |
| **Total Accounts Receivable** | 610,502.93 |
| ▼ **Other Current Assets** | |
| 12000 · Undeposited Funds | 2,440.00 |
| 12100 · Inventory Asset | 30,683.38 |
| 12800 · Employee Advances | 832.00 |
| 13100 · Pre-paid Insurance | 4,050.00 |
| 13400 · Retainage Receivable | 3,703.02 |
| **Total Other Current Assets** | 41,708.40 |
| **Total Current Assets** | 720,284.12 |
| ▼ **Fixed Assets** | |
| 15000 · Furniture and Equipment | 34,326.00 |
| 15100 · Vehicles | 78,936.91 |
| 15200 · Buildings and Improvements | 325,000.00 |
| 15300 · Construction Equipment | 15,300.00 |
| 16900 · Land | 90,000.00 |
| 17000 · Accumulated Depreciation | -110,344.60 |
| **Total Fixed Assets** | 433,218.31 |
| ▼ **Other Assets** | |
| 18700 · Security Deposits | 1,720.00 |
| **Total Other Assets** | 1,720.00 |
| **TOTAL ASSETS** | **1,155,222.43** |
| ▼ **LIABILITIES & EQUITY** | |
| ▼ **Liabilities** | |
| ▼ **Current Liabilities** | |
| ▼ **Accounts Payable** | |
| 20000 · Accounts Payable | 26,636.92 |
| 20001 · Accounts Payable - CAD | 7,800.00 |
| 20002 · Accounts Payable - AUD | 45,472.00 |
| 20003 · Accounts Payable - EUR | 72,500.00 |

So we will want to create a Home Currency Valuation for the Canadian dollar, Euro, and the Australian dollar.

- Click on **Company > Manage Currency > Home Currency Adjustment**.
- Choose the valuation **date** of June 30.
- Select or enter the **Currency** from the drop-down. We'll do the Euro first
- The exchange rate for the euro as of June 30 appears, but we know that's not right, because this is far in the past and we haven't been updating the exchange rates that far back. We certainly never updated a rate for June 30 in particular. In fact, from looking at the Currency List, this is picking up the 1.45 rate from March 31, because that's the most recent rate for this date or earlier. The next date for which we have an exchange rate for this currency is July 1. So we need to overwrite this June 30 exchange rate with an agreed-upon rate for the end of June. Let's enter a rate of 1.2.
- Click on **Calculate Adjustment**.

- We see all balance sheet accounts with balances in euros as of that date. This can include banks, credit cards, accounts receivable, and accounts payable accounts. For receivables and payables, they are separated into individual euro customers' and vendors' balances.

- We see the existing foreign balance (euro), home currency balance (USD in this case), and, if this home currency adjustment is to be entered, what the adjusted home currency balance would be...along with the resulting gain or loss in the home currency.

- We can pick and choose which of these rows we want to include in our home currency adjustment. Normally, we'd choose all of them. I have seen people exclude certain rows from time to time if the amount of the gain or loss is minor. But we're going to choose them all. We enter a checkmark in the column for the all account balances in this currency that we want to revalue.

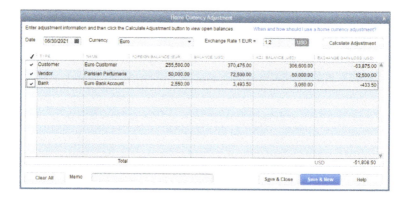

- Let's make this go through by selecting either **Save & Close** or **Save & New**.
- Now let's take a look at what this transaction did. Run a Transaction List by Date (**Reports > Accountant & Taxes > Transaction List by Date**) report and customize it for the one day of June 30. It's a General Journal!

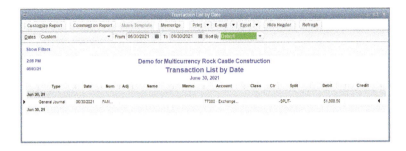

- Let's double-click on it to open up the general journal entry. To keep things easy to view, if we see previous journal entries, let's hide the list:

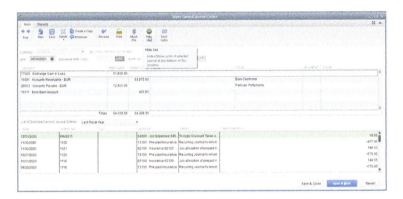

- That's easier to view! We'll probably want to change the entry number that was pre-populated by QuickBooks. But here's what's really interesting: if you look really hard, you can see, greyed out, the fact that this is a special type of journal entry - a Home Currency Adjustment! I'm saving the entry again to save the new number I gave it:

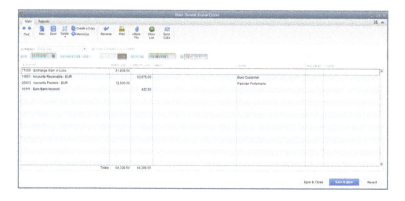

- I see that it's decreased the value of the Euro Receivable for Euro Customer by 63,875.00 in our home currency - that's a loss. It also decreased the value of the Euro Payables for the vendor Parisian Perfumerie by 12,500 - that's a gain. It's also decreased the value of the Euro Bank Account by 433.50 in our home currency - definitely a loss. If there were multiple euro customers and euro vendors that were having their balances revalued, they'd appear here as separate rows in this special journal entry. This is something that the rest of the time, QuickBooks Desktop does not allow you to do, having more than one accounts receivable and/or accounts payable row in a general journal entry. But this is a special case!
- Now let's look at the behind-the-scenes journal entry by looking at the **Transaction Journal** in the ribbon or by selecting **Control+Y**. Let's add columns for the currency, exchange rate, and foreign amount:

- You can see here that the actual euro amounts are unaffected; only the home currency value is affected! If this were a normal journal entry in which we debited and credited these accounts for these amounts, you'd see the foreign amount changing as well...in other words, we'd be changing the number of foreign currency units!

- But with a Home Currency Adjustment, we are changing the home currency value without changing the number of foreign currency units, so that future payments, calculations, and bank reconciliations are not jeopardized.

- To look into this from another angle, let's open the register for the Euro Accounts Receivable, Euro Accounts Payable, and the Euro Bank account: the June 30 balance in euros is unaffected because the Home Currency Adjustment transaction counts for 0 in foreign currency!

- Let's look at a Profit & Loss for June 30: there's a positive exchange gain or loss of $51,808.50..in other words, a loss!
- If we zoom in on that figure, we see that it's the sum of:
- Loss on Euro Accounts Receivable (debit) of $63,875
- Gain on Euro Accounts Payable (credit) of $12,500
- Loss on Euro Bank Account (debit) of $433.50
- Any open invoices or bills revalued as of that June 30 valuation date would now be considered as if they were entered with the new exchange rate of June 30.
- A Home Currency Adjustment's exchange rate for the valuation date does not appear on the Currency list for that currency and date.

The Australian and Canadian Home Currency Adjustments for June 30 can be created in exactly the same way; just be sure to enter the June 30 valuation date as well as the agreed-upon exchange rate for that currency on that date. We will cover an unusual situation for Home Currency Adjustments in which the foreign amount is zero in the next lesson.

## Enter the Home Currency Adjustment ASAP

But what if there were some previously-entered foreign bill payments, invoice payments, or deposits to a foreign bank that were dated *after* our valuation date, for example, in July? Any gains or losses automatically calculated by QuickBooks on those transactions entered in July before the Home Currency Adjustment would be based on the *original* exchange rates of the opening transactions such as bills and invoices.

The Home Currency Adjustment, if entered after those closing transactions but dated before them, would not affect those exchange gain/loss calculations. The home currency value of foreign accounts receivable and payable, as well as the exchange gain or loss, would be incorrect in that later month after the closing transactions.

An additional Home Currency Adjustment would revalue things properly, but that relies on the user remembering to create one in a timely fashion.

Also, there are cases I've seen of a foreign currency accounts receivable or payable account's subledger report (such as Open Invoices or Unpaid Bills Detail) not matching the amount on the Balance Sheet for the same date. This is linked at least in part to back-dated Home Currency Adjustments being entered after some foreign currency Pay Bills, Receive Payment, or Bank Deposits that are dated later. But we will cover a workaround for this problem later in this book.

*In any case, it's important to enter the Home Currency Adjustment as soon as possible at or after the milestone valuation date. Also, remember to create Home Currency Adjustments in chronological order: for example, if you're doing this monthly, create the Home Currency Adjustment for August 31 before you create one for September 30.*

## Return to the Exchange Gains or Losses Account

Now that we have covered Home Currency Adjustments, we can update what we know about the Exchange Gains or Losses account. It should contain only transactions that are of these types:

- Payment (i.e. invoice payment)
- Deposit (i.e. to the bank if an invoice is paid or a sales receipt is linked to Undeposited funds)
- Bill Payment (by check or credit card)
- General Journal (created by Home Currency Adjustment)

If there are any transactions in this account not of these types, some cleaning up of the company file is required. We'll get into this when we touch on fraud later in this book.

# Chapter 15

# Home Currency Adjustments when Foreign Balance = 0 (but Balance Sheet is not = 0)

## Where, oh Where did my Home Currency Adjustment Go?

There will be times when starting to create a Home Currency Adjustment will take you nowhere, because there is a zero foreign currency balance in an account, but the home currency balance is not zero.

I've seen this happen in client companies where they have closed out a foreign currency bank account, and so there are zero foreign currency units in that account and QuickBooks knows it. Regardless of swings in the exchange rate, everyone can agree that the home currency value of zero *in any currency* should always be zero.

But there will be times when the foreign balance is zero but the home currency balance on the Balance Sheet is not zero. When that happens, the regular Home Currency Adjustment steps discussed earlier will not even display that account to revalue, because its foreign balance is zero. We'll cover how this can happen and how to perform a workaround to address it.

## How can we have a zero foreign balance with a non-zero home currency balance?

Believe it or not, it's surprisingly easy for this scenario to happen.

Think of a very simple situation in a Multicurrency environment: we open a new foreign currency bank account.

Let's say on December 31, 2020, we opened a Brazilian Real bank account with 10,000 BRL.

At the rate of exchange on that day, the balance sheet showed a home currency value of $1,925.21 USD, because the Brazilian Real was worth $0.192521 US on that date, and that was the exchange rate used on the transaction.

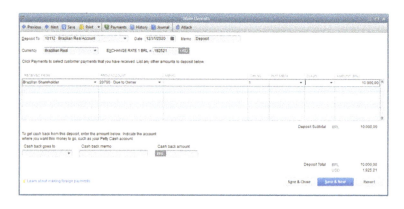

In this super-simple example, there are no bank charges or other transactions. In fact, we did nothing with this bank account during the next few months, until we decided on July 31, 2021 that it wasn't worth keeping and we transferred the 10,000 Brazilian Reals out and put them into the US Bank Account. We officially closed the Brazilian account.

But the exchange rate has changed by then, as exchange rates do; in fact, the Brazilian Real was worth $0.191835 US, according to the US Checking Account to which we transferred the funds on July 31, 2021 (that's how much they would give us for the Brazilian balance in the US Checking Account), and so that was the exchange rate we used on this second transaction.

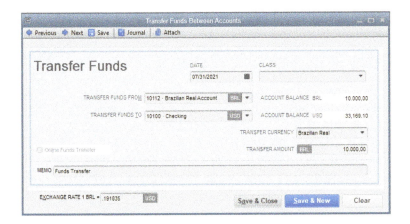

So, this transaction reduced the Brazilian Bank Account's balance by 10,000 BRL, or $1,918.35 USD.

Do you see what happened?

On December 31, 2020, the BRL bank's register showed 10,000 BRL , but the home currency value on the Balance Sheet was $1,925.21 USD.

After the account was closed on July 31, 2021, the BRL bank's register showed 0 BRL.

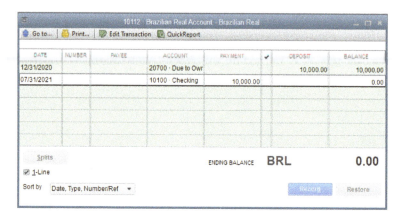

…but the home currency value of that Brazilian Bank Account on the Balance Sheet was $6.86 USD ($1,925.21 less $1,918.35). We see that in the Account QuickReport:

We can add more columns to this QuickReport for Currency, Exchange Rate, and Foreign Amount:

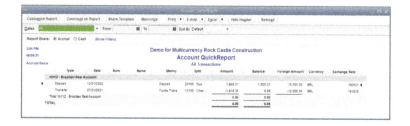

If we look at the Balance Sheet for August 31, we see that the closed Real Account has a non-zero home currency balance:

So that's how a zero balance in a foreign currency can yield a non-zero balance on the Balance Sheet. I used a very simple example with two transactions. You can imagine how a real company with multiple transactions in foreign currencies over time at different rates of exchange can get messed up.

## What is the Home Currency Adjustment experience with a foreign balance of zero?

When we realize that the fluctuating exchange rates are the culprit, the next step is generally to create a Home Currency Adjustment (HCA) by selecting **Company > Manage Currency > Home Currency Adjustment**. Then specify the valuation date (August 31, 2021) and the currency (Brazilian Real); then enter an agreed-upon exchange rate for this date: 0.1935 (although the exchange rate really doesn't matter when the foreign amount is zero). We would be looking to see $0.00 in the *Adj. Balance (USD)* column.

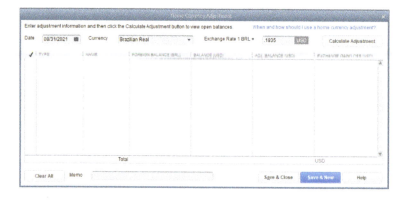

But when we hit **Calculate Adjustment**, the Brazilian Real Account doesn't appear. In fact, in this simple example, we see this message:

Why?

The answer is simple. When the *Home Currency Adjustment* window is launched, it looks for non-zero foreign balances to revalue. (Think of all the foreign bank accounts, credit cards, and more importantly, customers and vendors for each currency that the software would have to go through in calculating the amount of the HCA in a normal company file; the developers obviously decided to minimize the computing power required by telling QuickBooks to ignore zero foreign balances.) So Quick-Books ignores any foreign balances that are zero, such as the Brazilian Real Account in the simple example above, when it is about to create a Home Currency Adjustment revaluation transaction.

## Solution: Back-door method of creating home currency adjustments

But I have a back-door workaround. Home Currency Adjustments created in the conventional way above, result in, behind the scenes, a very specific type of General Journal Entry: it's one in which the debits or credits affect the foreign accounts (even multiple A/R customers and A/P vendors in one transaction, normally not possible in QuickBooks Desktop), the flip side affects the *Exchange Gain or Loss* account, and the *Home Currency Adjustment* box in the header section of the entry is automatically checked. This results in the number of foreign monetary units being unchanged (so reconciliations in that currency are unaffected), but the home currency value is changed, with the difference booked to *Exchange Gain or Loss*.

So this workaround is to open a new General Journal Entry, and leave the *Currency* and *Exchange Rate* fields untouched. (The *Exchange Rate* will display 1 anyway in a Home Currency Adjustment.) Then check the *Home Currency Adjustment* box in the header, enter the valuation date (August 31, 2021 in this case), specify the foreign bank account (the *Brazilian Real Account* in this example) and the amount of the value adjustment (credit of $6.86 in this case to zero out the value), and on the second line, specify the *Exchange Gain or Loss* account and balance the entry (debit $6.86 in this case).

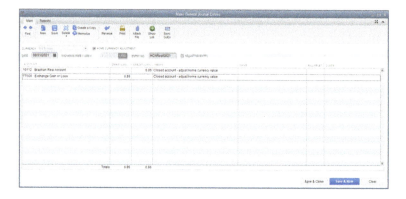

After doing this, the Brazilian Real Account's balance in Reals is still 0, but its home currency value is now correct at $0 US. The Brazilian Real Account has disappeared from the Balance Sheet, and the $6.86 in Exchange Gain or Loss credit resulted in $6.86 in Net Income for the day:

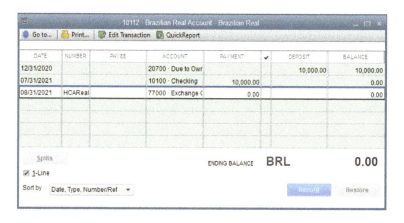

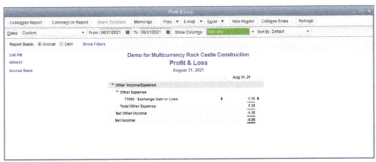

This General Journal Entry trick is useful whenever you close or zero out the balance on a foreign bank or credit card account.

And, keep in mind that Home Currency Adjustments should be entered in the conventional way (**Company > Manage Currency > Home Currency Adjustment**) whenever possible because it's easy to use. But keep this General Journal Entry method in mind for 0 foreign balances with non-zero home currency values appearing on the Balance Sheet.

# Chapter 16
# Selling in Foreign Currency: Maintaining Foreign Price Lists

## How QuickBooks Desktop deals with items sold in foreign currency

The best way to illustrate how QuickBooks deals with items sold in foreign currency is to demonstrate. Let's create a scenario.

First, let's create a generic Service item that has a default selling price of 100. Remember: the selling price when we set up an item is denominated in our home currency. Let's make it non-taxable to simplify things. It doesn't matter what we call it or the account to which we map it. Click **OK**.

Now we know that when we sell this item, the price of 100 pops up on sales forms such as invoices, sales receipts, and credit memos. Also, estimates and sales orders will have this price pop up.

But what if we're selling it to a foreign customer? That's a different story.

Here, we're selling to a Euro Customer on August 5. As soon as we enter the Generic Service item and hit the TAB key to go to the next fields, notice that the price of the item pops up - but not at $100.

The default price we see is $100 on August 5, converted into the foreign currency of Euros at the exchange rate QuickBooks has in place for that date.

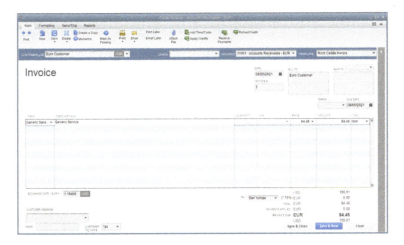

If we change the date of the invoice to January 1, we see this Exchange Rates pop-up window telling us that a different date will necessitate a new exchange rate. We click **OK**:

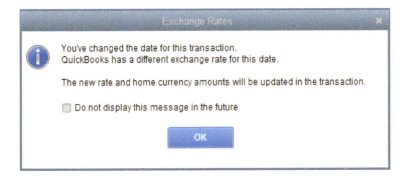

The price in euros should change, but it's not...let's just add a new line item for the Generic Service. I'll delete the first row and now we see the new rate:

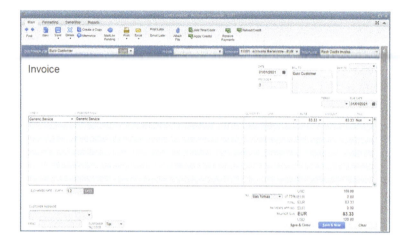

Also, if I click on the drop-down beside the rate, I see this list of pre-existing price level prices converted into euros at the rate of exchange on the date of this invoice.

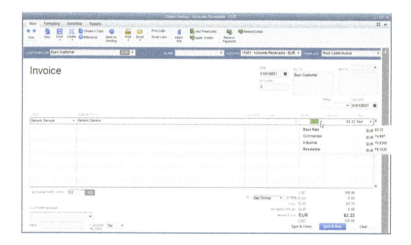

The bottom line here is that unless we do something about it, the foreign selling price of anything we sell will fluctuate with the exchange rate.

Otherwise, the user has to remember to overwrite the default fluctuating euro price on every invoice for every item. This could lead to errors and bad customer relations.

We need a way to produce static foreign selling prices that do not fluctuate with the exchange rate.

## Creating static foreign selling prices

### Step 1: Price level creation for the foreign currency

To create static foreign selling prices, we need to use Per Item Price Levels, which are available in QuickBooks Desktop Premier, Accountant, and Enterprise. QuickBooks Desktop Pro will not help us here, as it only allows for Fixed Percentage Price Levels.

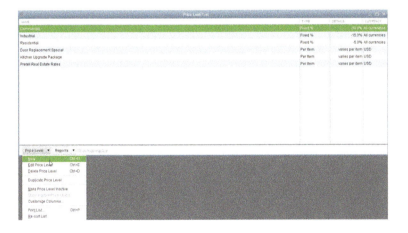

Let's create a new Price Level. We'll call it *Euro Standard* and make it a **Per Item** type. We specify that it's for the **Euro** currency.

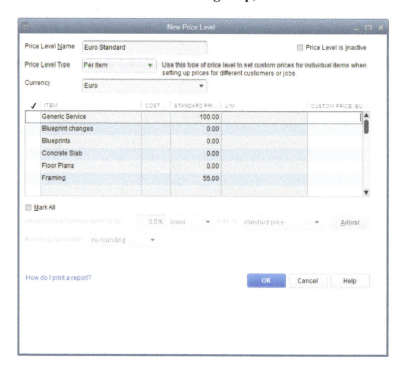

Let's put in the euro price for just one item to illustrate: the Generic Service item.

Do not check the left column next to the item; just enter the desired euro default selling price.

The custom price in euros, regardless of the exchange rate, is €90. Let's click **OK**. Do not click Adjust, even if you are asked if you want to adjust the prices.

### Step 2: Price level associated with foreign customers

Creating the price level is fine, and that means we can choose the static foreign price from the drop-down next to the rate in the invoice. But let's make this more automatic and associate this price level with any Euro customers: open the customer, and, in the **Payment Settings** tab, choose the new price level from the Price Level drop-down. Then click **OK**.

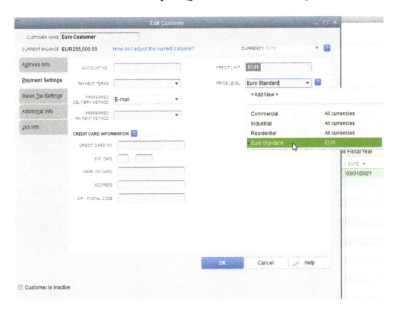

We can do this for *de Gaulle, Charles* as well or...we can create another different euro price level for members of government. That's right; we can create several per item price levels per currency. So let's leave Charles de Gaulle alone.

Now let's go back and invoice Euro Customer:

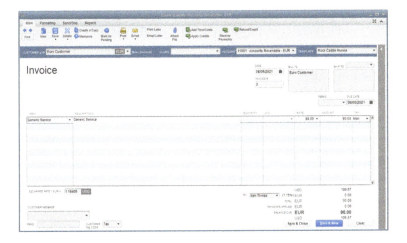

The 90 euro price is the default now because we've created the per item price level and we've associated it with this customer. Any other customers in euros, if they haven't been given a per item price level for this currency, will have a fluctuating selling price.

In addition, the Euro Standard price level price is now available to select from the drop-down for the rate if we are invoicing a euro customer and we forgot to give them this price level:

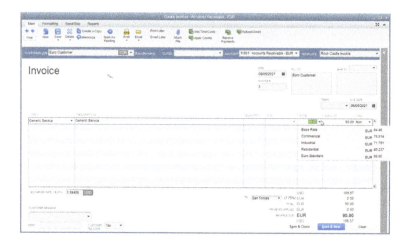

But again, this is more prone to errors if we are depending on every user remembering to overwrite a price or choose from a drop-down.

Therefore, the best course of action is to use QuickBooks Desktop Premier, Accountant, or Enterprise, create per item price levels for each foreign currency, and remember to associate each foreign customer with the correct price level in the Payment Settings.

The currency price level's prices that we've associated with a foreign customer will pop up as the default selling price for any items specified in that price level on invoices, credit memos, sales orders, and estimates.

## Tracking billable time for foreign customers

Although we have an elegant workaround for setting static foreign prices, there is a glitch in QuickBooks Desktop that is a problem when tracking billable time for foreign customers.

Again, let's demonstrate.

Let's track 10 hours of billable time on January 1 performed by Dan Miller for Euro Customer:

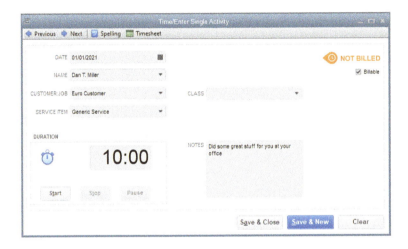

Let's choose **Save & Close**.

Now let's invoice the Euro Customer. As soon as we enter the name and hit the TAB key, we get this Billable Time/Costs window:

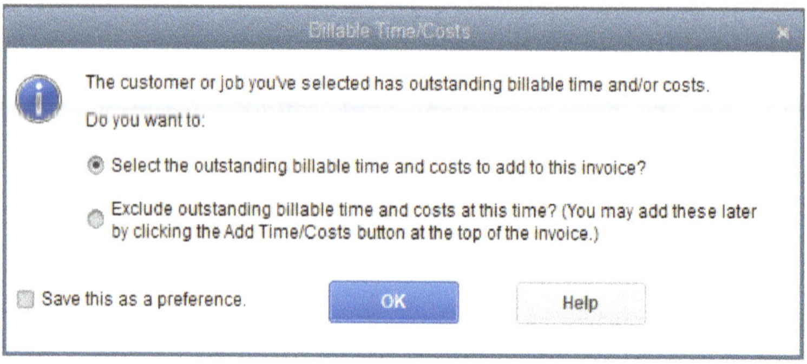


Let's choose **OK**, indicating we want to select outstanding billable time and costs to the invoice. The Choose Billable Time and Cost window then appears, and we check that we want to add the 10 billable hours of Generic Service we just tracked:

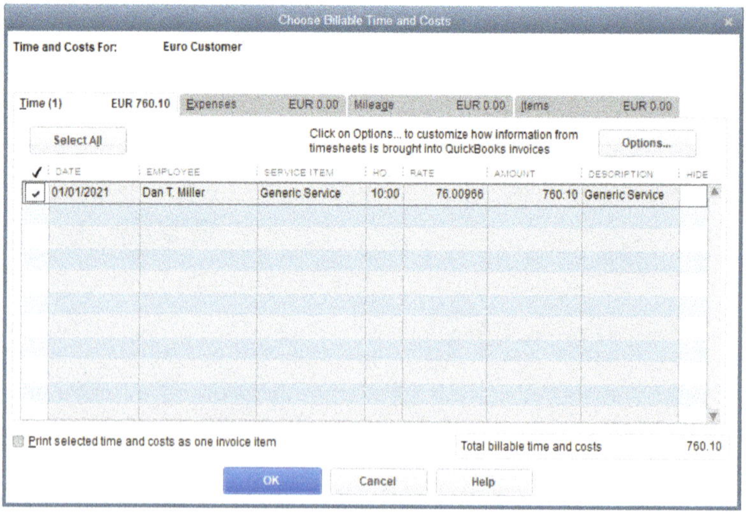


Before we click **OK** to add the billable time to the invoice, do you see the problem? The selling price of the Generic Service item for Euro Customer is coming through at 76.00966, the equivalent of $100, the original price in the home currency, on the date of the invoice at the rate of exchange that QuickBooks offers for that date.

**Multicurrency in QuickBooks® Desktop**

Let's click **OK**.

Sure enough, the invoice populates with the billable time's selling price of €76.00966 each. Let's test this out further. Let's go to the next vacant line and manually add the Generic Service item separately and see what QuickBooks does:

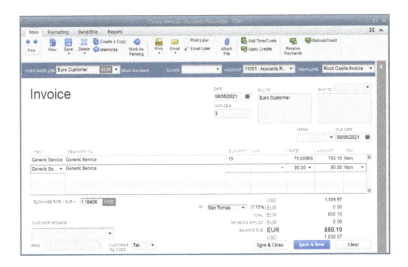

Sure enough, the row with the manually added Generic Service automatically populates with the 90 euro price, even before we add the number of hours.

## What's the bottom line for tracking billable foreign time?

Therefore, for tracking billable time for foreign customers that will come over onto invoices, you have to remember to overwrite the offered selling price with the proper selling price that would come over if you hadn't tracked the time and just entered the time manually on the invoice.

Another option is to enter the time as Not Billable. Then run a *Time by Job Detail* report and filter it for Not Billable time (and memorize it to make it easier to run in the future) and for foreign customers (you'll need to filter by customer name). Run this report at whatever frequency you deem necessary, but keep it consistent (for example, once a month or twice a month on the 15th and the last day).

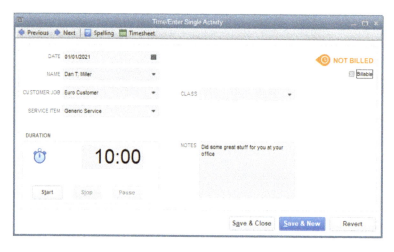

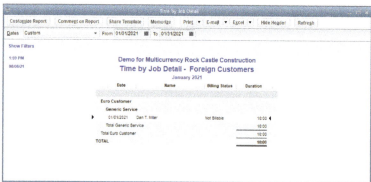

Then, from that report, manually enter an invoice to each foreign customer with Not Billable time listed on the report. Although you have to enter the time yourself, at least the selling price will populate correctly.

## Billable foreign costs

We covered billable time for foreign customers. But what about billable costs?

Let's use our Generic Service item again. We're buying 100 hours of this Generic Service at $35 each, the default per unit purchase cost in our home currency, and we're specifying the Euro Customer and that these are billable to that customer. Let's **Save & Close**.

Now let's invoice our Euro Customer, who is associated with the Euro Standard price level, in which Generic Service has a euro selling price of €90.

As soon as we start to invoice the Euro Customer, we get this Billable Time/Costs message, and we choose to **Select the outstanding billable time and costs to add to this invoice**. We then click **OK**.

We then click on the **Items** tab in the *Choose Billable Time and Costs* window. We place a checkmark next to the Generic Service, and then we choose **OK**.

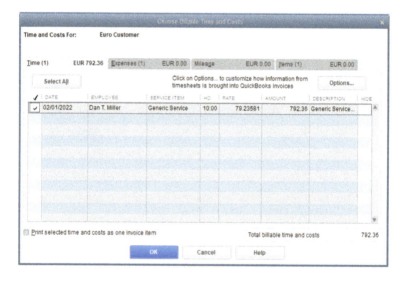

But notice that the rate for this Generic Service is €79.23581, not €90. QuickBooks is picking up the default home currency selling price and converting it to euros at the prevailing rate of exchange on the date of the invoice.

That means we have to overwrite the per unit euro selling price so that €90 appears!

## What's the bottom line for tracking billable costs for foreign customers?

Therefore, for tracking billable costs for foreign customers that will come over onto invoices, you have to remember to overwrite the offered selling price with the proper selling price that would come over if you hadn't tracked the billable costs and just entered the time manually on the invoice.

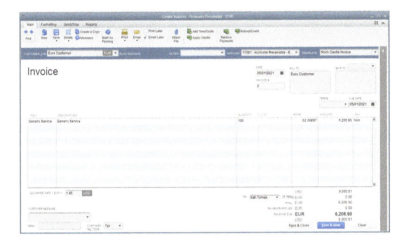

Another option is to mark the items as Not Billable on the purchase transaction, but still associate the cost with the customer.

Then run an Unbilled Costs by Job report and filter it for Not Billable time (and memorize it to make it easier to run in the future) and foreign customers (you'll need to filter by customer name). (If you filter by currency, you'll only see vendor transactions wherein the vendor is in that same currency.) Add columns for Item and Qty. Run this report at whatever frequency you deem necessary, but keep it consistent (for example, once a month or twice a month on the 15th and the last day).

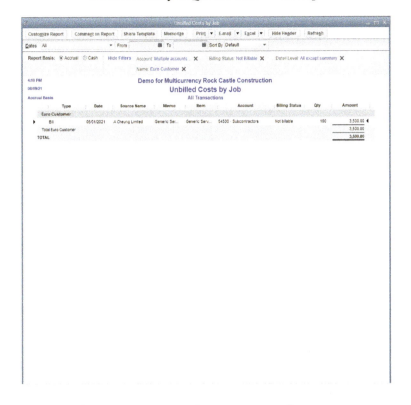

Then use this report to enter the items manually into an invoice for this customer, and the proper price level will take over.

It's a pain, I know.

# Chapter 17
# Purchase Orders and Purchasing in a Multicurrency Environment

While QuickBooks Desktop has created a nifty method of establishing foreign selling prices that don't vary with the exchange rate (see the previous lesson for more information), we don't have anything so elegant for establishing fixed foreign purchase costs. (Price Levels apply to selling prices rather than purchase costs.)

## Foreign purchase orders and bills using items

That means that when we want to purchase an item from a foreign vendor, the default per unit purchase cost is the foreign currency equivalent of whatever the home currency default cost for that item is, and that will vary with fluctuations in the exchange rate.

The following demonstration uses purchase orders, but can also be used for bills that use the *Items* tab.

Let's go back to our Generic Service item and turn it into a two-sided one: check the box next to **This service is used in assemblies or is performed by a subcontractor or partner**. Then we add details in the *Purchase Information* section. We'll give it a default unit purchase cost value of $35 (that's our home currency) and the expense account will be *54500 Subcontractors*. Let's click **OK** to save this. I'll say **No** to updating existing transactions since I know there were none on the purchase side of things using this item.

Now let's create a new Euro vendor and we'll call him or her *Euro Subcontractor*. We assign him or her the Euro currency and select **OK**.

Now let's issue a purchase order to this subcontractor, asking them for 100 hours of Generic Service.

When I start to enter the Generic Service item, the default rate, which is the per unit purchase cost in that currency, is really weird. It is, in fact, the $35 default home currency per unit cost expressed in the euro currency at the prevailing rate of exchange on this date.

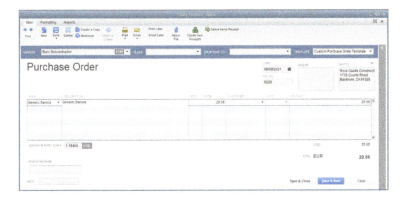

If we change the date, we get this Exchange Rates window, indicating that the exchange rate will change for a different date:

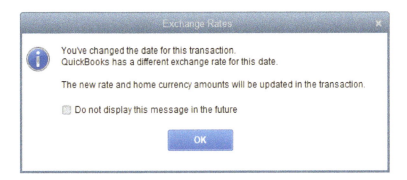

The cost in euros didn't change on row 1. However, if we added another row with the same Generic Service item, the rate on the new row does indeed change:

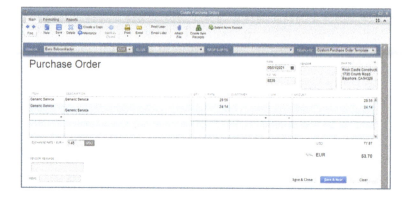

Either way, the per unit cost on the Generic Service is incorrect and will continue to fluctuate with the exchange rate. We can, of course, overwrite it on an individual purchase order:

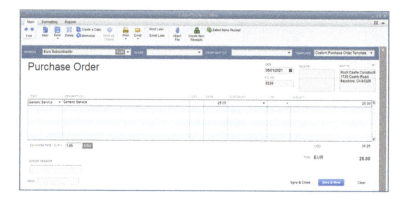

This is what we are advised to do by Intuit Tech Support, but that means that this is prone to user error.

## Workarounds for foreign purchase orders and bills

There are a couple of workarounds for this issue, however.

## Workaround #1

If we know that the purchase order to various Euro vendors for the time being will be for the Generic Service item at 25 euros per hour, we can populate a PO with this information (and memorize it):

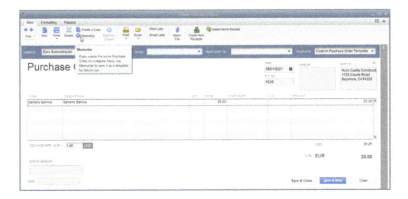

We name it something like "Generic Service PO Euro." As this is a foreign currency transaction, QuickBooks does not allow this to be an automated memorized transaction or part of a group. But that's fine because we want to choose the **Do Not Remind Me** option and then click **OK**.

We don't have to save the original purchase order if we're just setting up the memorized transaction. So when we close it, we get this Recording Transaction screen. We select **No**.

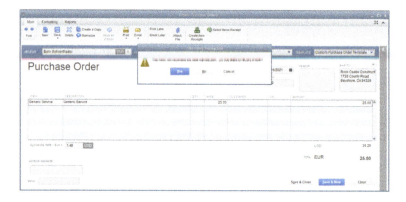

Now let's say that at some point in the future, we want to issue a PO to one of many euro currency vendors for this item. We simply go to the list of Memorized Transactions and double-click on the Generic Service PO Euro transaction, which is denominated in Euros:

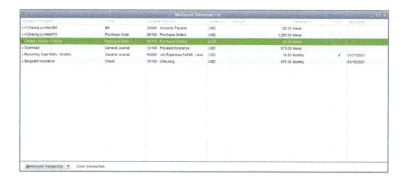

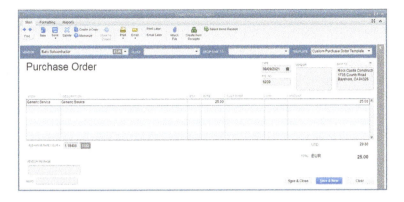

The PO appears with the correct currency and per unit cost in that currency. Even if we change the date, the quantity, and the vendor (to another euro vendor name), the per unit cost is unchanged:

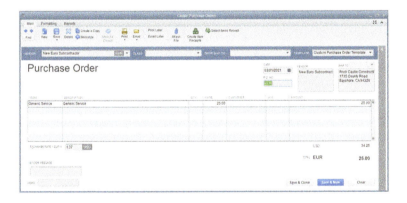

This was a very simple example. But imagine instead of one item on this PO, there are 20 items with the foreign per unit cost set up for each of them….and we memorized it just as we did with this one! We could bring up the memorized euro PO, change the vendor name if necessary, change the date and the quantities (and even delete rows that we don't need on the actual purchase order if we're not ordering everything), and issue the PO to the foreign vendor!

## Workaround #2

Another quick workaround is to take a pre-existing purchase order in foreign currency and, if it contains all the items we want to re-order, click on **Create a Copy** in the top **Main** ribbon.

The new purchase order will be pre-populated with the items and their per unit purchase costs in that currency.

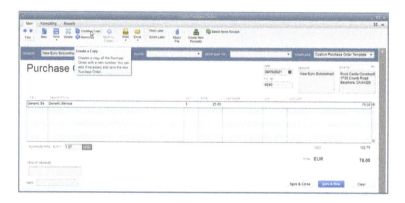

Make any necessary changes to the purchase order, such as the vendor, date, quantities and deleting rows for items that are not being ordered, and then save the PO and submit it to the foreign vendor.

When the bill arrives, QuickBooks reminds us that this vendor has one or more outstanding purchase orders. We specify that yes, the purchase order should populate the bill...and the proper per unit cost and quantity appear!

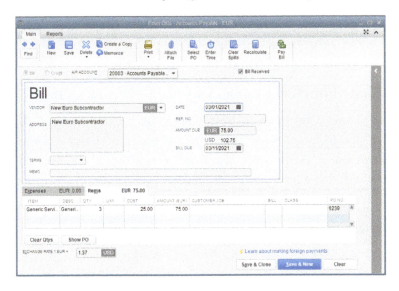

That's great if we are using purchase orders to populate our bills. But what if we are using foreign bills without creating purchase orders first?

The same two methodologies can work on bills without bringing purchase orders into the workflow. Use one of them:

1. Create a foreign bill using a foreign vendor, populated manually with the correct items and per unit purchase costs, then memorize the bill so that it sits on the list of memorized transactions to be used in the future. If the bill we were creating was just a template and not an actual bill at the time, we can escape out of the bill and not record it. When using the foreign bill from the memorized transactions list, change the date, quantities, and vendor if needed; delete any rows that are unnecessary in the new bill.

2. Find a previously-entered foreign bill using the items and per unit foreign costs and copy it to create a new bill with the items and costs. Change the date,

quantities, and vendor if needed; delete any rows that are unnecessary in the new bill.

## What about foreign checks and credit card charges?

Fortunately, the same two workarounds available for foreign bills on their own or foreign bills from purchase orders also apply to checks and credit card charges, whether on their own or connected to a foreign purchase order.

## Item pricing and costs in foreign currency

The examples we worked with earlier in this lesson used two-sided service items. Let's try using an inventory item. Let's use Light Pine Cabinets:

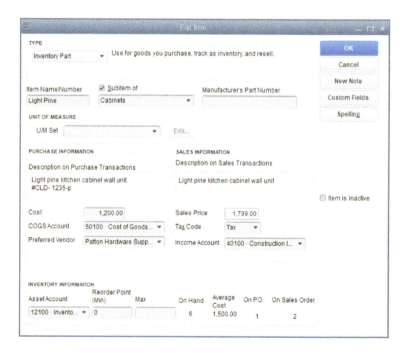

Also, we've edited the Euro Standard price level to incorporate a default euro selling price for this item: €1,500.

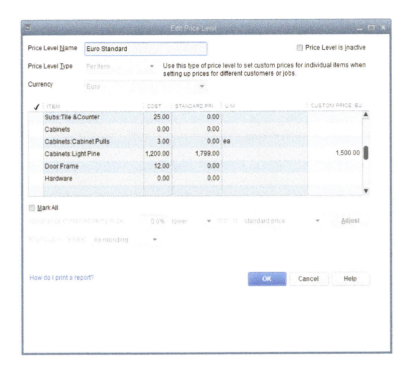

Remember, we can't create a default purchase cost for an item using Price Levels.

Let's buy 100 Light Pine Cabinets from Europe from the Euro Subcontractor on May 1. We have not created a memorized transaction for the purchase, and we haven't created a prior transaction using the correct purchase costs that we can copy. The default home currency purchase cost expressed in euros appears, so we need to overwrite it.

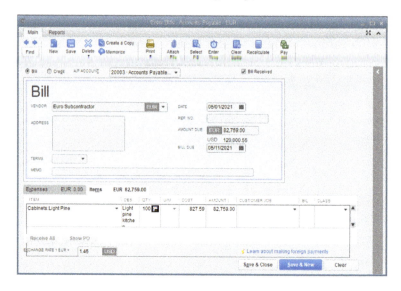

Let's overwrite the per unit purchase cost in euros to €1,000 each. Let's specify the Euro Customer and (since we learned our lesson about billable costs for foreign customers), we won't make this billable. **Save & Close**.

Now let's invoice the Euro Customer on May 1 as well for these items.

Because we are invoicing a customer who does not have billable costs (we took out the "billable" checkmark on the bill), we don't see a Billable Time/Costs message.

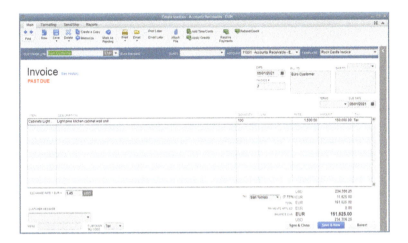

Then we use a Unbilled Costs by Job report, filtered for Unbillable (and maybe filter for the various foreign customers as well) to see the 100 Light Pine Cabinets for this customer. So we add these items manually to the invoice and the Euro Standard Price Level price appears properly. Let's **Save & Close**.

Now the reporting in foreign currency falls apart.

If we run an Inventory Valuation Detail for just May 1, we see amounts in the home currency, and there is no option for adding or substituting foreign currency columns and amounts:

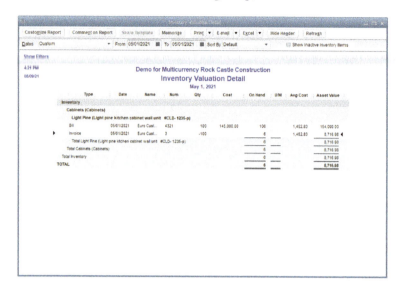

If we run an Item Profitability for May 1, we get numbers in the home currency with no option to add foreign currency amounts as well:

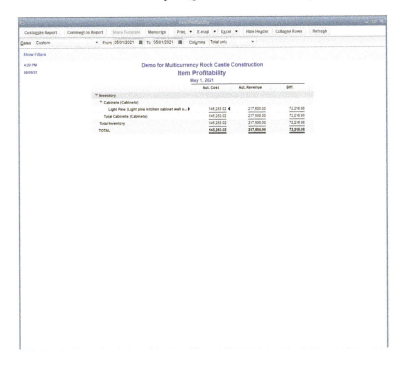

We'd need to drill down into each number to get a detailed report and add foreign currency columns. Here, we drill down into the **Actual Cost** number and add a column for Foreign Amount:

We do the same with the **Actual Revenue** number:

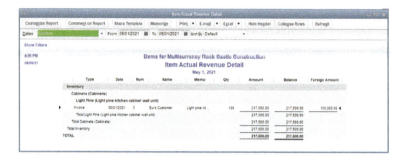

All these detail reports would have to be exported to Excel and reformatted in order to make sense out of profitability in another currency. It can be a colossal mess!

However, keep in mind that what counts is how profitable these purchases and sales are in the end in our own home currency...so the home currency reports do serve a very important purpose. And if we are sustaining a loss on a particular item, it makes sense to raise the price in all currencies...or stop selling it!

# Module 4: Multicurrency Reporting & Troubleshooting in QuickBooks Desktop

# Chapter 18
# Reporting in Multicurrency

## Multicurrency is in the details

Most reporting in QuickBooks Desktop will be in the home currency, and in order to see foreign currency amounts we have to ask for it in the form of customizations.

As we covered earlier in this book, foreign currency amounts do not display in summary reports such as the Profit & Loss Standard and the Balance Sheet Standard. Summary reports display home currency total amounts only. Account by account, both the Profit & Loss and the Balance Sheet display the sum of home currency amounts for all transactions included in the reporting period.

So let's say that there are two invoices for Demolition Income for €1,000 each on two different dates: January 1 and July 1. On January 1, the €1,000 invoice is worth $1,200, and on July 1, the €1,000 invoice is worth $1,215.67. If there are no other invoices affecting Demolition Income, the Profit & Loss Standard report will display $2,415.67 for Demolition Income for the year: the sum of home currency equivalents (at the time of each transaction, given the rate of exchange) of all foreign currency transactions affecting this account.

## Demo for Multicurrency Rock Castle Construction
## Profit & Loss
### January through December 2021

|  | Jan - Dec 21 |
|---|---|
| **▼ Ordinary Income/Expense** | |
| **▼ Income** | |
| **▼ 40100 · Construction Income** | |
| 40110 · Design Income | 78,360.00 |
| 40130 · Labor Income | 439,495.00 |
| 40140 · Materials Income | 217,500.00 ◀ |
| 40150 · Subcontracted Labor Income | 2,700.00 |
| Total 40100 · Construction Income | 738,055.00 |
| 40101 · Demolition Income | 2,415.67 |
| Total Income | 740,470.67 |
| **▼ Cost of Goods Sold** | |
| 50100 · Cost of Goods Sold | 145,283.02 |
| **▼ 54000 · Job Expenses** | |
| 54500 · Subcontractors | 143.00 |
| Total 54000 · Job Expenses | 143.00 |
| Total COGS | 145,426.02 |
| **Gross Profit** | 595,044.65 |
| **▼ Expense** | |
| 5578 · Promotion | 72,500.00 |
| 5643 · Consulting | 53,272.00 |
| **▼ 63600 · Professional Fees** | |
| 63610 · Accounting | 750.00 |
| Total 63600 · Professional Fees | 750.00 |
| Total Expense | 126,522.00 |
| Net Ordinary Income | 468,522.65 |
| **▼ Other Income/Expense** | |
| **▼ Other Expense** | |
| 77000 · Exchange Gain or Loss | 51,431.86 |
| Total Other Expense | 51,431.86 |
| Net Other Income | -51,431.86 |
| **Net Income** | **417,090.79** |

If you want to see the original foreign currency amounts, you can drill down on the summary figures in the summary report, or you can run a detailed version of the report, such as a Profit & Loss Detail or a Balance Sheet Detail.

Here, we are drilling down on one account, the Demolition Income account. We've added a column for the Foreign Amount and the Foreign Balance:

Demo for Multicurrency Rock Castle Construction
Transaction Detail By Account
January through December 2021

| Type | Date | Num | Adj | Name | Memo | Class | Clr | Split | Debit | Credit | Balance | Foreign Amount | Foreign Balance |
|------|------|-----|-----|------|------|-------|-----|-------|-------|--------|---------|----------------|-----------------|
| **40101 · Demolition Income** | | | | | | | | | | | | | |
| Invoice | 01/01/2021 | 4 | | Euro Customer | Demolition | | | 11001 · Acco... | | 1,200.00 | 1,200.00 | 1,000.00 | 1,000.00 |
| Invoice | 07/01/2021 | 5 | | Euro Customer | Demolition | | | 11001 · Acco... | | 1,215.67 | 2,415.67 | 1,000.00 | 2,000.00 |
| Total 40101 · Demolition Income | | | | | | | | | 0.00 | 2,415.67 | 2,415.67 | | 2,000.00 |
| TOTAL | | | | | | | | | 0.00 | 2,415.67 | 2,415.67 | | 2,000.00 |

Or, we could have drilled down on the total income figure from the Profit & Loss Standard and added those two columns for the Foreign Amount and the Foreign Balance:

Demo for Multicurrency Rock Castle Construction
Transaction Detail By Account
January through December 2021

| Type | Date | Num | Adj | Name | Memo | Class | Clr | Split | Debit | Credit | Balance | Foreign Amount | Foreign Balance |
|------|------|-----|-----|------|------|-------|-----|-------|-------|--------|---------|----------------|-----------------|
| **40100 · Construction Income** | | | | | | | | | | | | | |
| **40110 · Design Income** | | | | | | | | | | | | | |
| Invoice | 01/01/2021 | 1 | | de Caulle, Charles | Floor plans | | | 11001 · Acco... | | 360.00 | 360.00 | 300.00 | 300.00 |
| Invoice | 03/31/2021 | 1 | | Canuck Candies | Blueprints | | | 11002 · Acco... | | 78,500.00 | 78,360.00 | 150,500.00 | 150,500.00 |
| Total 40110 · Design Income | | | | | | | | | 0.00 | 78,360.00 | 78,360.00 | | 150,300.00 |
| **40130 · Labor Income** | | | | | | | | | | | | | |
| Invoice | 03/31/2021 | 2 | | Euro Customer | Installation la... | | | 11001 · Acco... | | 370,475.00 | 370,475.00 | 305,500.00 | 305,500.00 |
| Invoice | 05/31/2021 | 1 | | Outback Odysseys | Framing labor | | | 11001 · Acco... | | 69,020.00 | 439,495.00 | 35,000.00 | 340,500.00 |
| Total 40130 · Labor Income | | | | | | | | | 0.00 | 439,495.00 | 439,495.00 | | 340,500.00 |
| **40140 · Materials Income** | | | | | | | | | | | | | |
| Invoice | 05/01/2021 | 3 | | Euro Customer | Light pine lit... | | | 11001 · Acco... | | 217,500.00 | 217,500.00 | 150,500.00 | 150,000.00 |
| Total 40140 · Materials Income | | | | | | | | | 0.00 | 217,500.00 | 217,500.00 | | 150,000.00 |
| **40150 · Subcontracted Labor Income** | | | | | | | | | | | | | |
| Invoice | 01/01/2021 | 1 | | de Caulle, Charles | Install tile or... | | | 11001 · Acco... | | 2,700.00 | 2,700.00 | 2,250.00 | 2,250.00 |
| Total 40150 · Subcontracted Labor Income | | | | | | | | | 0.00 | 2,700.00 | 2,700.00 | | 2,250.00 |
| Total 40100 · Construction Income | | | | | | | | | 0.00 | 738,055.00 | 738,055.00 | | 643,050.00 |
| **40101 · Demolition Income** | | | | | | | | | | | | | |
| Invoice | 01/01/2021 | 4 | | Euro Customer | Demolition | | | 11001 · Acco... | | 1,200.00 | 1,200.00 | 1,000.00 | 1,000.00 |
| Invoice | 07/01/2021 | 5 | | Euro Customer | Demolition | | | 11001 · Acco... | | 1,215.67 | 2,415.67 | 1,000.00 | 2,000.00 |
| Total 40101 · Demolition Income | | | | | | | | | 0.00 | 2,415.67 | 2,415.67 | | 2,000.00 |
| TOTAL | | | | | | | | | 0.00 | 740,470.67 | 740,470.67 | | 645,050.00 |

Of course, we could also drill down on the Net Income figure from the Profit & Loss Standard and add those two columns. But it's easier to run a Profit & Loss Detail report.

Here, in the Profit & Loss Detail report, we've added a Foreign Amount column and Foreign Balance column.

Demo for Multicurrency Rock Castle Construction
**Profit & Loss Detail**
January through December 2021

| Type | Date | Num | Adj | Name | Memo | Class | Clr | Split | Debit | Credit | Balance | Foreign Amount | Foreign Balance |
|------|------|-----|-----|------|------|-------|-----|-------|-------|--------|---------|----------------|-----------------|
| **Ordinary Income/Expense** | | | | | | | | | | | | | |
| **Income** | | | | | | | | | | | | | |
| **40100 · Construction Income** | | | | | | | | | | | | | |
| **40110 · Design Income** | | | | | | | | | | | | | |
| Invoice | 01/01/2021 | 1 | | de Gaulle, Charles | Floor plans | | | 11000 · Acco | | 360.00 | 360.00 | 300.00 | 300.00 |
| Invoice | 03/21/2021 | 1 | | Canuck Candies | Blueprints | | | 11002 · Acco | | 78,000.00 | 78,360.00 | 100,000.00 | 100,300.00 |
| Total 40110 · Design Income | | | | | | | | | 0.00 | 78,360.00 | 78,360.00 | | 100,300.00 |
| **40130 · Labor Income** | | | | | | | | | | | | | |
| Invoice | 03/21/2021 | 2 | | Euro Customer | Installation la | | | 11000 · Acco | | 370,475.00 | 370,475.00 | 255,500.00 | 255,500.00 |
| Invoice | 03/21/2021 | 1 | | Outback Odysseys | Framing labor | | | 11000 · Acco | | 68,020.00 | 438,495.00 | 85,000.00 | 340,500.00 |
| Total 40130 · Labor Income | | | | | | | | | 0.00 | 438,495.00 | 438,495.00 | | 340,500.00 |
| **40140 · Materials Income** | | | | | | | | | | | | | |
| Invoice | 06/01/2021 | 2 | | Euro Customer | Light pine kit | | | 11000 · Acco | | 217,500.00 | 217,500.00 | 150,000.00 | 150,000.00 |
| Total 40140 · Materials Income | | | | | | | | | 0.00 | 217,500.00 | 217,500.00 | | 150,000.00 |
| **40150 · Subcontracted Labor Income** | | | | | | | | | | | | | |
| Invoice | 01/01/2021 | 1 | | de Gaulle, Charles | Install tile or | | | 11000 · Acco | | 2,700.00 | 2,700.00 | 2,250.00 | 2,250.00 |
| Total 40150 · Subcontracted Labor Income | | | | | | | | | 0.00 | 2,700.00 | 2,700.00 | | 2,250.00 |
| Total 40100 · Construction Income | | | | | | | | | 0.00 | 738,095.00 | 738,095.00 | | 593,050.00 |
| **40901 · Demolition Income** | | | | | | | | | | | | | |
| Invoice | 01/01/2021 | 4 | | Euro Customer | Demolition | | | 11000 · Acco | | 1,200.00 | 1,200.00 | 1,500.00 | 1,500.00 |
| Invoice | 07/01/2021 | 5 | | Euro Customer | Demolition | | | 11000 · Acco | | 1,215.67 | 2,415.67 | 1,500.00 | 2,500.00 |
| Total 40901 · Demolition Income | | | | | | | | | 0.00 | 2,415.67 | 2,415.67 | | 2,500.00 |
| Total Income | | | | | | | | | 0.00 | 740,470.67 | 740,470.67 | | 595,000.00 |
| **Cost of Goods Sold** | | | | | | | | | | | | | |
| **50100 · Cost of Goods Sold** | | | | | | | | | | | | | |
| Invoice | 06/01/2021 | 2 | | Euro Customer | Light pine kit | | | 11000 · Acco | 145,282.02 | | 145,282.02 | 100,195.19 | 100,195.19 |
| Total 50100 · Cost of Goods Sold | | | | | | | | | 145,282.02 | 0.00 | 145,282.02 | | 100,195.19 |
| **64000 · Job Expenses** | | | | | | | | | | | | | |
| **64500 · Subcontractors** | | | | | | | | | | | | | |

Notice that in the Foreign Amount column, there are no subtotals or totals and here's why. The transactions here include those of all currencies, including the home currency. The Foreign Amount column will house the amounts in the original currency, even if it's the home currency. Any subtotals or totals in the Foreign Amount column will be a total of all transactions in that section, and will likely display a meaningless total of amounts in different currencies.

In fact, even in the Foreign Balance column, the subtotals are meaningless. Let's add a Currency column to illustrate. Look at the Labor Income transactions. One is in Euros and the other is in Australian Dollars. The original foreign amounts are €255,500 and $85,000 in Australian Dollars. The subtotal of the Foreign Balance column for this account is the meaningless total of 340,500, as if the two currencies were at par with each other.

Demo for Multicurrency Rock Castle Construction
**Profit & Loss Detail**
January through December 2021

| Type | Date | Num | Adj | Name | Memo | Class | Clr | Split | Debit | Credit | Balance | Foreign Amount | Currency | Foreign Balance |
|---|---|---|---|---|---|---|---|---|---|---|---|---|---|---|
| **Ordinary Income/Expense** | | | | | | | | | | | | | | |
| **Income** | | | | | | | | | | | | | | |
| **40100 · Construction Income** | | | | | | | | | | | | | | |
| **40110 · Design Income** | | | | | | | | | | | | | | |
| Invoice | 01/01/2021 | 1 | | de Gaulle, Charles | Floor plans | | 11001 · Acco... | | | 500.00 | 500.00 | 500.00 | EUR | 100.00 |
| Invoice | 03/14/2021 | 1 | | Canuck Candles | Blueprints | | 11002 · Acco... | | | 78,100.00 | 78,300.00 | 100,000.00 | CAD | 100,100.00 |
| Total 40110 · Design Income | | | | | | | | 0.00 | | 78,300.00 | 78,300.00 | | | 100,200.00 |
| **40130 · Labor Income** | | | | | | | | | | | | | | |
| Invoice | 02/21/2021 | 2 | | Euro Customer | Installation la... | | 11001 · Acco... | | | 370,475.00 | 370,475.00 | 265,500.00 | EUR | 265,500.00 |
| Invoice | 05/31/2021 | 1 | | Outback Odysseys | Framing labor | | 11003 · Acco... | | | 89,020.00 | 459,495.00 | 85,300.00 | AUD | 340,500.00 |
| Total 40130 · Labor Income | | | | | | | | 0.00 | | 459,495.00 | 459,495.00 | | | 348,600.00 |
| **40140 · Materials Income** | | | | | | | | | | | | | | |
| Invoice | 05/01/2021 | 3 | | Euro Customer | Light pine kit... | | 11001 · Acco... | | | 217,500.00 | 217,500.00 | 150,500.00 | EUR | 150,500.00 |
| Total 40140 · Materials Income | | | | | | | | 0.00 | | 217,500.00 | 217,500.00 | | | 150,500.00 |
| **40150 · Subcontracted Labor Income** | | | | | | | | | | | | | | |
| Invoice | 01/01/2021 | 1 | | de Gaulle, Charles | Install tile or... | | 11001 · Acco... | | | 2,700.00 | 2,700.00 | 2,250.00 | EUR | 2,250.00 |
| Total 40150 · Subcontracted Labor Income | | | | | | | | 0.00 | | 2,700.00 | 2,700.00 | | | 2,250.00 |
| Total 40100 · Construction Income | | | | | | | | 0.00 | | 738,995.00 | 738,995.00 | | | 591,380.00 |
| Invoice | 01/01/2021 | 4 | | Euro Customer | Demolition | | 11001 · Acco... | | | 1,200.00 | 1,200.00 | 1,500.00 | EUR | 1,500.00 |
| Invoice | 07/01/2021 | 3 | | Euro Customer | Demolition | | 11001 · Acco... | | | 1,215.67 | 2,415.67 | 1,000.00 | EUR | 2,500.00 |
| Total 40101 · Demolition Income | | | | | | | | 0.00 | | 2,415.67 | 2,415.67 | | | 2,500.00 |
| Total Income | | | | | | | | 0.00 | | 740,479.67 | 740,479.67 | | | 558,050.00 |
| **Cost of Goods Sold** | | | | | | | | | | | | | | |
| **50100 · Cost of Goods Sold** | | | | | | | | | | | | | | |
| Invoice | 05/01/2021 | 3 | | Euro Customer | Light pine kit... | | 11001 · Acco... | 145,283.02 | | 145,283.02 | 100,195.19 | EUR | 100,195.19 |
| Total 50100 · Cost of Goods Sold | | | | | | | | | 145,283.02 | 0.00 | 145,283.02 | | | 100,195.19 |

Here's something we can do, however. It can be done either in the Profit & Loss Standard or the Profit & Loss Detail report: filter currency by currency.

So let's start with the Profit & Loss Standard report. Let's filter it for the Euro currency only. As with any report that is being filtered, it's a good idea to show the filters as well as edit the Header/Footer on the report:

Currency: Euro ✕          Date: This Fiscal Year ✕

### Demo for Multicurrency Rock Castle Construction
### Profit & Loss - Euro only
#### January through December 2021

| | Jan - Dec 21 |
|---|---|
| ▼ Ordinary Income/Expense | |
| ▼ Income | |
| ▼ 40100 · Construction Income | |
| 40110 · Design Income | 360.00 |
| 40130 · Labor Income | 370,475.00 |
| 40140 · Materials Income | 217,500.00 |
| 40150 · Subcontracted Labor Income | 2,700.00 |
| Total 40100 · Construction Income | 591,035.00 |
| 40101 · Demolition Income | 2,415.67 |
| Total Income ▶ | 593,450.67 ◀ |
| ▼ Cost of Goods Sold | |
| 50100 · Cost of Goods Sold | 145,283.02 |
| ▼ 54000 · Job Expenses | |
| 54500 · Subcontractors | 143.00 |
| Total 54000 · Job Expenses | 143.00 |
| Total COGS | 145,426.02 |
| Gross Profit | 448,024.65 |
| ▼ Expense | |
| 5578 · Promotion | 72,500.00 |
| Total Expense | 72,500.00 |
| Net Ordinary Income | 375,524.65 |
| ▼ Other Income/Expense | |
| ▼ Other Expense | |
| 77000 · Exchange Gain or Loss | -433.50 |
| Total Other Expense | -433.50 |
| Net Other Income | 433.50 |
| Net Income | 375,958.15 |

Now this report displays the results of Euro currency transactions during the period. We can run a Profit & Loss Detail filtered for Euro transactions only or we can drill down on the Net Income figure.

Let's go with the Profit & Loss Detail report filtered only for Euro transactions, and add a column for the Foreign Amount and the Foreign Balance. Let's add a column for the currency just to be sure we got our filters right.

Yes, we can move the columns around and take away some that we don't need. So I'm getting rid of a few columns to make it easier on the eyes:

Now the Foreign Balance subtotals and totals actually mean something, as long as we've filtered for one currency at a time. They are the totals for Euros in this case.

If this is a report that will be run time and time again, it's a good idea to memorize it, along with any similar reports for other currencies.

Let's scroll down to the Exchange Gain or Loss account. Notice that, as a result of transactions being closed (bills being paid or invoice payments received and put into the bank), there is a balance in this account in the home currency. But there is no foreign currency equivalent - it's all zeroes. And that makes sense. Exchange gains and losses are calculated based on the home currency and the change in value of foreign currency transactions as exchange rates fluctuate.

rs   Account: All income/expense accounts ✕      Currency: Euro ✕      Date: This Fiscal Year ✕

**Demo for Multicurrency Rock Castle Construction**
**Profit & Loss Detail - Euro Only**
January through December 2021

| Type | Date | Num | Name | Debit | Credit | Balance | Foreign Amount | Currency | Foreign Balance |
|---|---|---|---|---|---|---|---|---|---|
| Invoice | 05/01/2021 | 3 | Euro Customer | | 217,500.00 | 217,500.00 | 150,000.00 | EUR | 150,000.00 |
| Total 40140 · Materials Income | | | | 0.00 | 217,500.00 | 217,500.00 | | | 150,000.00 |
| 40150 · Subcontracted Labor Income | | | | | | | | | |
| Invoice | 01/01/2021 | 1 | de Gaulle, Charles | | 2,700.00 | 2,700.00 | 2,250.00 | EUR | 2,250.00 |
| Total 40150 · Subcontracted Labor Income | | | | 0.00 | 2,700.00 | 2,700.00 | | | 2,250.00 |
| Total 40100 · Construction Income | | | | 0.00 | 591,035.00 | 591,035.00 | | | 408,050.00 |
| 40101 · Demolition Income | | | | | | | | | |
| Invoice | 01/01/2021 | 4 | Euro Customer | | 1,200.00 | 1,200.00 | 1,000.00 | EUR | 1,000.00 |
| Invoice | 07/01/2021 | 5 | Euro Customer | | 1,215.67 | 1,215.67 | 1,000.00 | EUR | 2,000.00 |
| Total 40101 · Demolition Income | | | | 0.00 | 2,415.67 | 2,415.67 | | | 2,000.00 |
| Total Income | | | | 0.00 | 593,450.67 | 593,450.67 | | | 410,050.00 |
| Cost of Goods Sold | | | | | | | | | |
| 50100 · Cost of Goods Sold | | | | | | | | | |
| Invoice | 05/01/2021 | 3 | Euro Customer | 145,283.02 | | 145,283.02 | 100,195.19 | EUR | 100,195.19 |
| Total 50100 · Cost of Goods Sold | | | | 145,283.02 | 0.00 | 145,283.02 | | | 100,195.19 |
| 54000 · Job Expenses | | | | | | | | | |
| 54500 · Subcontractors | | | | | | | | | |
| Bill | 03/01/2021 | 1234 | Euro Subcontractor | 34.25 | | 34.25 | 25.00 | EUR | 25.00 |
| Bill | 05/01/2021 | 1234 | New Euro Subcon... | 108.75 | | 143.00 | 75.00 | EUR | 100.00 |
| Total 54500 · Subcontractors | | | | 143.00 | 0.00 | 143.00 | | | 100.00 |
| Total 54000 · Job Expenses | | | | 143.00 | 0.00 | 143.00 | | | 100.00 |
| Total COGS | | | | 145,426.02 | 0.00 | 145,426.02 | | | 100,295.19 |
| Gross Profit | | | | 145,426.02 | 593,450.67 | 448,024.65 | | | 309,754.81 |
| Expense | | | | | | | | | |
| 5578 · Promotion | | | | | | | | | |
| Bill | 03/01/2021 | 78978 | Parisian Perfumerie | 72,500.00 | | 72,500.00 | 50,000.00 | EUR | 50,000.00 |
| Total 5578 · Promotion | | | | 72,500.00 | 0.00 | 72,500.00 | | | 50,000.00 |
| Total Expense | | | | 72,500.00 | 0.00 | 72,500.00 | | | 50,000.00 |
| Net Ordinary Income | | | | 217,926.02 | 593,450.67 | 375,524.65 | | | 259,754.81 |
| Other Income/Expense | | | | | | | | | |
| Other Expense | | | | | | | | | |
| 77000 · Exchange Gain or Loss | | | | | | | | | |
| Payment | 02/15/2021 | 1234 | de Gaulle, Charles | | 637.50 | -637.50 | | EUR | 0.00 |
| Deposit | 02/20/2021 | | | 204.00 | | -433.50 | | EUR | 0.00 |
| Total 77000 · Exchange Gain or Loss | | | | 204.00 | 637.50 | -433.50 | | | 0.00 |
| Total Other Expense | | | | 204.00 | 637.50 | -433.50 | | | 0.00 |
| Net Other Income | | | | 204.00 | 637.50 | 433.50 | | | 0.00 |
| Net Income | | | | 218,130.02 | 594,088.17 | 375,958.15 | | | 259,754.81 |

As I said earlier, most of the reporting in QuickBooks Desktop requires that we ask the program via customizations to provide us with original foreign amounts.

We did this by choosing **Control+Y** or **Reports > Transaction Journal** at the top of a transaction to get the Transaction Journal behind the scenes, and then we added our desired columns. Here, we've added the Foreign Amount, Currency, and Exchange Rate columns to this invoice:

Demo for Multicurrency Rock Castle Construction
Transaction Journal
All Transactions

| Trans # | Type | Date | Num | Name | Memo | Account | Class | Debit | Credit | Foreign Amount | Currency | Exchange Rate |
|---------|------|------|-----|------|------|---------|-------|-------|--------|----------------|----------|---------------|
| ▶ 1706 | Invoice | 03/31/2021 | 2 | Euro Customer | | 11001  Accounts | | 370,475.00 | | 255,500.00 | EUR | 1.45 ◀ |
| | | | | Euro Customer | Installation la | 40130  Labor Inco | | | 370,475.00 | -255,500.00 | EUR | 1.45 |
| | | | | State Board of Equ... | CA sales tax ... | 25500  Sales Tax ... | | 0.00 | | 0.00 | EUR | 1.45 |
| | | | | | | | | 370,475.00 | 370,475.00 | | | |
| TOTAL | | | | | | | | 370,475.00 | 370,475.00 | | | |

## Where do foreign amounts appear by default?

But there are a couple of exceptions to this, where QuickBooks offers up the foreign amount without us asking for it.

## Foreign account registers

One exception happens when we look at a foreign account's register, such as a foreign bank account.

When I double-click on the Euro Bank Account in the Chart of Accounts, after I view this warning that foreign currency registers cannot be edited directly and I choose **OK**,...

....I see the amounts only in the foreign currency from each transaction:

Yes, there's a 0 transaction here, but we never delete it: it's our home currency adjustment that revalues the foreign balance as of a certain date. While it doesn't affect the number of foreign currency units in this account, it does affect the home currency unit value.

Along the same lines, when we reconcile a foreign-denominated account, such as this bank account, we see only the foreign amounts from each transaction:

And since this window is not needlessly complicated with home currency equivalents, we can reconcile this account using the original foreign currency amounts and balances, straight off the bank statement in that currency.

One thing to remember here is that the 0 transaction from the home currency adjustment should be reconciled. It doesn't affect the totals, so it certainly doesn't hurt to reconcile it. And not reconciling it makes it more vulnerable to deletion by someone who doesn't know what they're doing.

There is another place where we don't have to ask QuickBooks Desktop to provide us with original currency foreign amounts: the Unrealized Gains and Losses report. We'll get to that later in this lesson.

Now, let's take a look at some other reports involving foreign currency.

## Receivables reports

If you're looking to see accounts receivable in the original foreign currencies, remember that QuickBooks displays only the total of home currency values in summary reports - unless you do something about it.

So if you run an A/R Aging Summary report or a Customer Balance Summary report, you'll see the words "(Values in Home Currency)" appended to the titles.

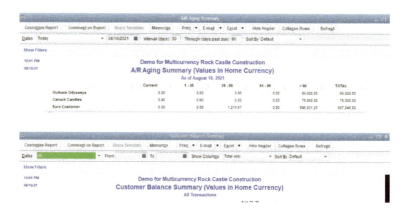

But you can change this to the transaction currency on each by selecting **Customize Report > Display amounts in The Transaction Currency > OK**.

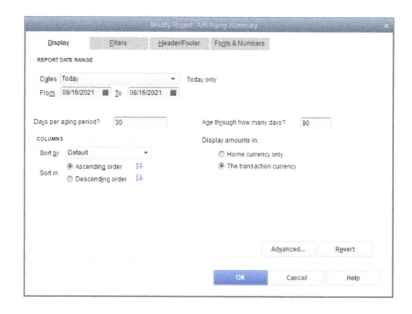

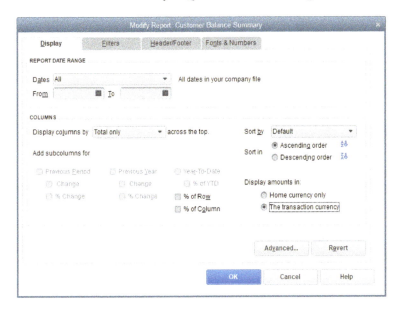

Then, you'll see the titles change to reflect the fact that the values are in the original transaction currency. You'll also see the name of the currency in brackets next to each customer.

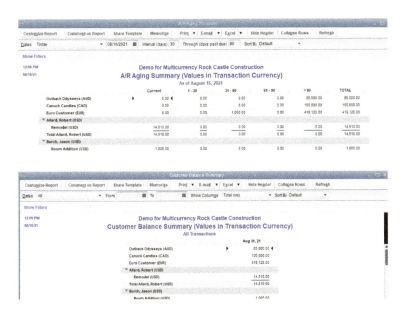

For receivables reports that start off with details, such as the Customer Balance Detail, A/R Aging Detail, and the Open Invoices reports, you can customize any of them to add the Currency, Exchange Rate, Foreign Amount, and the Foreign Open Balance.

However, if you're looking at more than one currency's receivables at a time, the total in the Foreign Open Balance column will be meaningless as it is a summary of different currency amounts, including the home currency (for which the foreign open balance amount is the same as the open balance amount).

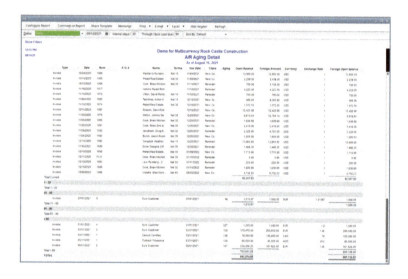

There is something that can be done, however. Let's start with the Open Invoices report. Let's filter it for one currency at a time (or we could filter the report for each receivables account, but this is easier especially if there is more than one accounts receivable account for a particular currency), and starting with the home currency, let's keep the columns as is except to add a column for the currency. We change the Header/Footer to reflect that it's only the home currency customers we are displaying here. Let's memorize it.

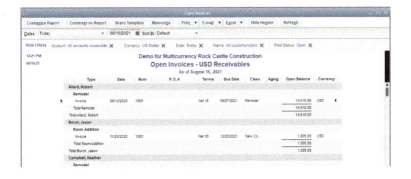

Next, let's change the currency filter to our first foreign currency. Then we change the Header/Footer to reflect which currency is being displayed, keep a column for the Currency, then add a column for the Foreign Amount and the Foreign Open Balance. We can remove the Open Balance column, which is the home currency value. We're displaying the filters just to be careful.

We memorize this one as well, and we repeat this for all currencies in which we are tracking foreign receivables. Receivables reports can be grouped together in the Memorized Reports area and run all at once.

Keep in mind that if we remove the filter for the currency and change the Header/Footer so that this displays all receivables, the total for the Foreign Open Balance column at the very bottom is absolutely meaningless.

## Payables reports

Everything we covered for Receivables reports also applies to Payables reports. The A/P Aging Summary and the Vendor Balance Summary reports can be customized to display the amounts in the transaction currency.

For payables reports that start off with details, such as the Vendor Balance Detail, A/P Aging Detail, and the Unpaid Bills Detail reports, you can customize any of them to add the Currency, Exchange Rate, Foreign Amount, and the Foreign Open Balance.

The home currency Unpaid Bills Detail report is easy enough to do. Just filter for the home currency (or the payables account(s) for that currency), change the Header/Footer, add a column for the Currency, and you've got it! Just memorize it.

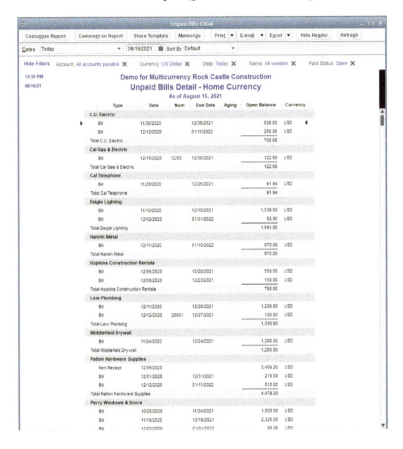

Then, the foreign payables reports can be filtered for any other currency (or payables accounts), and as long as we edit the Header/Footer to reflect the filter and show the filters as well, we can segregate the reporting of payables by currency.

It's easiest for me to view when I use the Unpaid Bills Detail report. Each of these can be customized and memorized, and the memorized payables reports can be put into a group so that all payables reports in all currencies can be run at once.

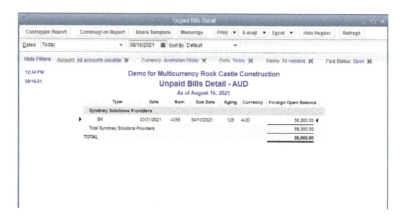

Keep in mind that if we remove the filter for the currency and change the Header/Footer so that this displays all payables, the total for the Foreign Open Balance column at the very bottom is absolutely meaningless.

## Realized Gains & Losses report

To find out what went into the realized gains and losses, select **Reports > Company & Financial > Realized Gains & Losses.**

You'll see all the "closing" of transactions that make QuickBooks Desktop automatically calculate and record gains and losses on foreign exchange transactions, as well as general journal entries that are actually home currency adjustments. The default date range for this report is All dates, but we can change it to focus on any date range we want:

Don't be thrown off by the totals of the column. They are confusing more than anything else. The Balance column is a running total of the Realized Gain/Loss amounts, where the total in the Realized Gain/Loss column is misleading.

In this report, we have an invoice payment, a deposit of that payment into the bank, a bill payment, and two home currency adjustments. You can tell they are home currency adjustments when you open each one because the grayed-out Home Currency Adjustment checkbox is checked by the system. This means that each entry is not adjusting any foreign-denominated amounts, only the foreign balance's value in the home currency per our example of stuffing foreign money in a mattress.

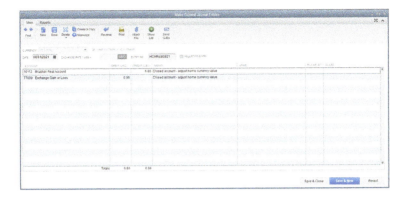

And, to be thorough, if we open up a Profit & Loss Standard report for the same period and if we look at the Exchange Gain or Loss amount, we see that it matches the final amount in the Balance column on the Realized Gains & Losses report.

## Unrealized Gains & Losses report

There are times when foreign currency amounts have not yet been revalued in the home currency, and we want to see what the potential gain and/or loss on foreign balances on the balance sheet would be.

That's when we run an Unrealized Gains & Losses report by selecting **Reports > Company & Financial > Unrealized Gains & Losses**.

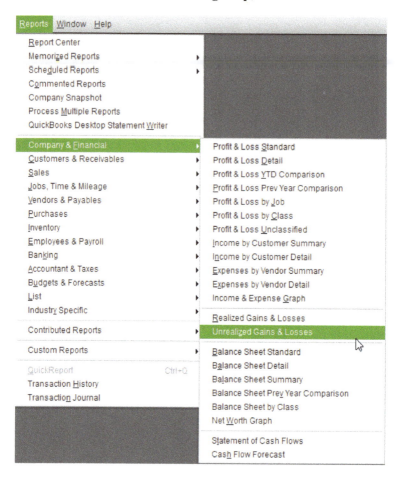

The next thing we see is a window in which we specify the "as of" date for which we want to see the report, and also all foreign currencies in use and the exchange rate we want to use on the "as of" date to calculate the potential gains and losses.

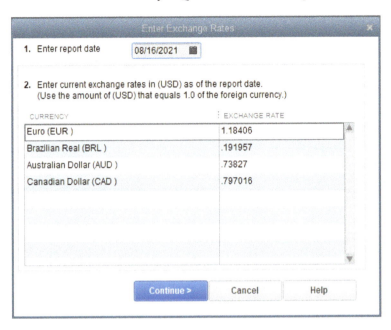

Let's enter the valuation date and the chosen exchange rates for each of our foreign currencies. We are using rather simple exchange rates, with only 3 significant digits.

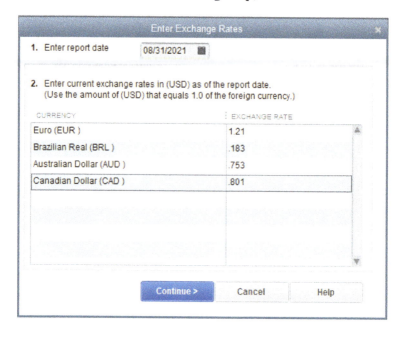

Let's hit **Continue**.

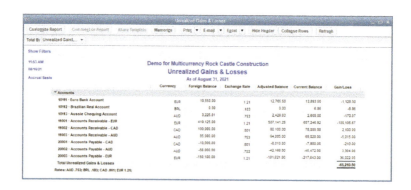

We see each currency and foreign balance for all the relevant accounts in the foreign currency - so we don't have to ask Quick-Books Desktop to provide us with these foreign amounts.

We also see the chosen exchange rate and what the new balance would be for each account if we revalued the foreign account using these exchange rates. We also see the current balance in the home currency - i.e., what's appearing on the Balance Sheet on the "as of" date.

And finally, comparing the potential Adjusted Balance to the Current Balance, we see what kind of Gain or Loss we would sustain.

This report has no effect or impact on our financial records. We don't see these figures in our Trial Balance, Balance Sheet, or Profit & Loss reports.

However, if we go ahead and perform a home currency adjustment for each of these currencies and for all the relevant accounts on this "as of" date using these exchange rates, our Exchange Gain or Loss account will be affected by exactly these amounts.

So the Unrealized Gains & Losses report is essentially a "crystal ball" into a "what if" situation.

## Exchange Gain or Loss account

While it's easy enough to view the Exchange Gain or Loss amount in the Profit & Loss for a period, it's also easy to find the Exchange Gain or Loss account on the Chart of Accounts and run a QuickReport for All dates.

This will list all the realized exchange gain or loss amounts resulting from paying a foreign bill, receiving payment on a foreign invoice, depositing that payment into the bank, and finally home currency adjustments.

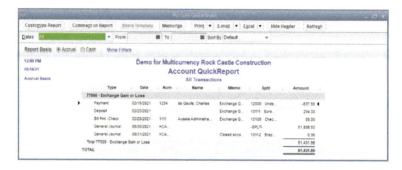

I encourage you to experiment with the reports that are easiest for you to view and consume, and try out adding new columns, changing the Header/Footer, and filtering to get exactly what you want to see.

# Chapter 19
# Discrepancies in Foreign Currency A/R and A/P Subledger Reports

I haven't had this happen often, but there have been times when an Accounts Receivable or Payable subledger report in a foreign currency doesn't match to its Balance Sheet counterpart for the same date. This is linked at least in part to back-dated Home Currency Adjustments being entered after some foreign currency Pay Bills, Receive Payment, or Bank Deposits that are dated later. Everything was fine and lined up perfectly until Home Currency Adjustments were entered under certain circumstances; it's a very fragile environment, dealing with multicurrency.

Have no fear; there are workarounds to these obstacles.

For instance, take a look at this Balance Sheet and these balances for the various Accounts Receivable accounts in the home currency:

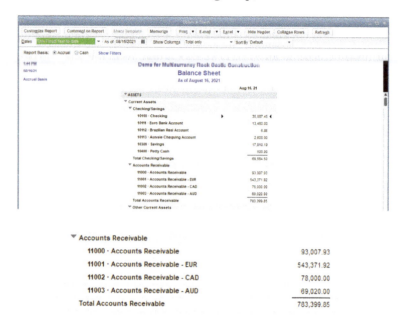

| Accounts Receivable | |
|---|---:|
| 11000 · Accounts Receivable | 93,007.93 |
| 11001 · Accounts Receivable - EUR | 543,371.92 |
| 11002 · Accounts Receivable - CAD | 78,000.00 |
| 11003 · Accounts Receivable - AUD | 69,020.00 |
| **Total Accounts Receivable** | 783,399.85 |

Now let's look at the various Accounts Receivable subledger reports, filtered for each currency. It so happens that the Euro report is the only one that doesn't match the balance sheet. It shows a home currency value on the same report date as $607,246.92, whereas the balance sheet indicates a balance of $543,371.92.

Let's look at the various Accounts Payable subledger reports, filtered for each currency. Again, it's the Euro report that doesn't match its counterpart on the balance sheet. It shows a home currency value on the same report date as $217,643.00, whereas the balance sheet indicates a balance of $205,143.00.

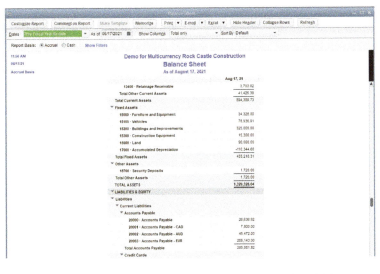

If this ever happens to you, do not worry. Assuming there is no data corruption, and that you're displaying both sets of reports for the same date, bear in mind that the **Balance Sheet figure is always correct**, and the problem with certain foreign currency A/R and A/P subledger reports is that Intuit engineers left out something in the default coding of those reports.

Let's review the various subledger reports and if they align with the balance sheet.

## Accounts receivable subledger reports

There are five main Accounts Receivable subledger reports:

- Customer Balance Summary (can be displayed either in the Home Currency or the original Transaction Currency)
- Customer Balance Detail
- A/R Aging Summary (can be displayed either in the Home Currency or the original Transaction Currency)
- A/R Aging Detail
- Open Invoices

## Customer Balance Summary in the Home Currency - matches the Balance Sheet

The Customer Balance Summary report can be displayed with values in the Home Currency or with values in the original Transaction Currency. Since we are dealing with matching the Balance Sheet, which always displays balances in the home currency, we're talking only about the Customer Balance Summary report displayed with values in the Home Currency.

This report will display the correct amount of receivables in the home currency, and it will match the Accounts Receivable balances on the Balance Sheet for the same date.

If you wish to see just a particular currency's accounts receivable reflected in this report, filter it for either the currency or the foreign accounts receivable account.

## Customer Balance Detail - matches the Balance Sheet

The Customer Balance Detail report will display the correct amount of receivables in the home currency, and it will match the Accounts Receivable balances on the Balance Sheet for the same date.

If you wish to see just a particular currency's accounts receivable reflected in this report, filter it for either the currency or the foreign accounts receivable account.

## A/R Aging Summary in the Home Currency - needs a tweak to match the Balance Sheet

The A/R Aging Summary report can be displayed with values in the Home Currency or with values in the original Transaction Currency. Since we are dealing with matching the Balance Sheet, which always displays balances in the home currency, we're talking only about the A/R Aging Summary report displayed with values in the Home Currency.

This report may not initially display the correct amount of receivables in the home currency. If it does not match, customize this report so that it is filtered for a **Paid Status = Either**. Then, it will match the Accounts Receivable balances on the Balance Sheet for the same date.

If you wish to see just a particular currency's accounts receivable reflected in this report, filter it for either the currency or the foreign accounts receivable account.

## A/R Aging Detail - needs a tweak to match the Balance Sheet

The A/R Aging Detail report may not initially display the correct amount of receivables in the home currency. If it does not match, customize this report so that it is filtered for a **Paid Status = Either**. Then, it will match the Accounts Receivable balances on the Balance Sheet for the same date.

If you wish to see just a particular currency's accounts receivable reflected in this report, filter it for either the currency or the foreign accounts receivable account.

## Open Invoices - may never match the Balance Sheet

The Open Invoices report may not display the correct amount of receivables in the home currency, and if that is the case, no amount of tweaking will get it to do so. That is a shame because it is usually my preferred A/R report of choice, but it falls apart sometimes when dealing with receivables in foreign currencies, even if it's filtered by account or currency.

## There is one more A/R report - The Collections Report

The Collections Report is generally not reviewed in comparison with the Balance Sheet. It also may not display home currency totals that match the balance sheet, and tweaking it with a filter of **Paid Status = Either** will make it match. However, considering its intended use, you will likely be changing the columns to display the Foreign Open Balance so that customers can be contacted and asked about upcoming payments of the correct amount in the correct currencies.

Here's a summary grid of the Accounts Receivable subledger reports and if or how they can match the Balance Sheet when foreign currencies and home currency adjustments might cause a discrepancy:

| Receivables Report: | Matches B/S | Matches B/S if Paid Status = Either | Tweaking won't help it match the B/S |
|---|---|---|---|
| Customer Balance Summary in Home Currency | ✓ | | |
| Customer Balance Detail | ✓ | | |
| A/R Aging Summary in Home Currency | | ✓ | |
| A/R Aging Detail | | ✓ | |
| Open Invoices | | | ✓ |

## Accounts payable subledger reports

There are five main Accounts Payable subledger reports:

- Vendor Balance Summary (can be displayed either in the Home Currency or the original Transaction Currency)
- Vendor Balance Detail
- A/P Aging Summary (can be displayed either in the Home Currency or the original Transaction Currency)
- A/P Aging Detail
- Unpaid Bills Detail

## Vendor Balance Summary in the Home Currency - matches the Balance Sheet

The Vendor Balance Summary report can be displayed with values in the Home Currency or with values in the original Transaction Currency. Since we are dealing with matching the Balance Sheet, which always displays balances in the home currency, we're talking only about the Vendor Balance Summary report displayed with values in the Home Currency.

This report will display the correct amount of payables in the home currency, and it will match the Accounts Payable balances on the Balance Sheet for the same date.

If you wish to see just a particular currency's accounts payable reflected in this report, filter it for either the currency or the foreign accounts payable account.

## Vendor Balance Detail - matches the Balance Sheet

The Vendor Balance Detail report will display the correct amount of payables in the home currency, and it will match the

Accounts Payable balances on the Balance Sheet for the same date.

If you wish to see just a particular currency's accounts payable reflected in this report, filter it for either the currency or the foreign accounts payable account.

## A/P Aging Summary in the Home Currency - needs a tweak to match the Balance Sheet

The A/P Aging Summary report can be displayed with values in the Home Currency or with values in the original Transaction Currency. Since we are dealing with matching the Balance Sheet, which always displays balances in the home currency, we're talking only about the A/P Aging Summary report displayed with values in the Home Currency.

This report may not initially display the correct amount of payables in the home currency. If it does not match, customize this report so that it is filtered for a **Paid Status = Either**. Then, it will match the Accounts Payable balances on the Balance Sheet for the same date.

If you wish to see just a particular currency's accounts payable reflected in this report, filter it for either the currency or the foreign accounts payable account.

## A/P Aging Detail - needs a tweak to match the Balance Sheet

The A/P Aging Detail report may not initially display the correct amount of payables in the home currency. If it does not match, customize this report so that it is filtered for a **Paid Status = Either**. Then, it will match the Accounts Payable balances on the Balance Sheet for the same date.

If you wish to see just a particular currency's accounts payable reflected in this report, filter it for either the currency or the foreign accounts payable account.

## Unpaid Bills Detail - may never match the Balance Sheet

The Unpaid Bills Detail report may not display the correct amount of payables in the home currency, and if that is the case, no amount of tweaking will get it to do so. That is a shame because it is usually my preferred A/P report of choice, but it falls apart sometimes when dealing with payables in foreign currencies, even if it's filtered by account or currency.

Here's a summary grid of the Accounts Payable subledger reports and if or how they can match the Balance Sheet when foreign currencies and home currency adjustments might cause a discrepancy:

Payables Report:

| Payables Report: | Matches B/S | Matches B/S if Paid Status = Either | Tweaking won't help it match the B/S |
|---|---|---|---|
| Vendor Balance Summary in Home Currency | ✔ | | |
| Vendor Balance Detail | ✔ | | |
| A/P Aging Summary in Home Currency | | ✔ | |
| A/P Aging Detail | | ✔ | |
| Unpaid Bills Detail | | | ✔ |

# Chapter 20
# Foreign Currency Accounting Entries at Year End

## I hate when accountants do this

Most accountants, if they're not working in the QuickBooks Desktop file directly (or using an Accountant's Copy), will provide a list of year-end adjusting journal entries for someone else to enter in QuickBooks at the client's site. Oftentimes these entries will include a revaluation of foreign currency account balances on the fiscal year end date.

I have found that these revaluation adjustments never take the multicurrency functionality of QuickBooks Desktop into account. Instead, these entries include either a debit or a credit to a foreign exchange adjunct account (for example: Euro Bank Account - FX) that is meant to be reported on right next to the original foreign account on the Balance Sheet. The flip side of the entry is to some exchange gain or loss account.

In fact, I have seen accountants who don't understand Quick-Books enter those very same adjustments directly into the QuickBooks Desktop file, and it messes up the bookkeeping.

This kind of treatment is fine, more or less, if a QuickBooks file is being used in which Multicurrency has not been enabled, but foreign balances need to be tracked. Frankly, I'd advise the business owner to have me convert them to Multicurrency.

## How should year end foreign currency adjustments be entered?

In QuickBooks Desktop files where Multicurrency has been enabled, I never enter these transactions the way they are laid out on the list of adjusting entries.

Instead, the accountant should have instructed the client to use the Home Currency Adjustment function, revaluing each foreign balance as of the fiscal year end at an agreed-upon rate of exchange.

If the rate of exchange is obvious from the memo for this entry, it is just fine to use Home Currency Adjustment.

If it's not obvious, you can go into that account register in QuickBooks and see what the foreign currency balance was on the year end date. Then, look at the balance on the pre-adjustment year end Balance Sheet, which is what QuickBooks believes that foreign balance is worth in the home currency. Do the math here and either add or subtract the adjustment amount the accountant specified, to see what the post-adjustment year end Balance Sheet figure will be. Then divide that post-adjustment Balance Sheet figure by the foreign currency balance to derive the effective exchange rate the accountant is using. Then use the Home Currency Adjustment.

A simpler thing to do if the accountant did not include the exchange rate in the memo to the adjustment is to create a journal entry with the Home Currency Adjustment box checked. Debit or credit the actual foreign account, and use the Exchange Gain/Loss account as the other side of the entry.

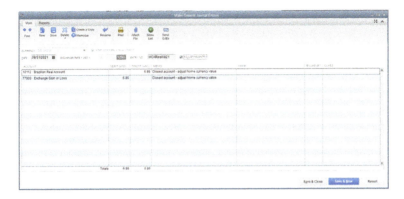

This back-door method of creating a Home Currency Adjustment was introduced in the lesson called *Home Currency Adjustments when Foreign Balance = 0 but Balance Sheet does not = 0.*

## Chapter 21
# Look at the Exchange Gain or Loss to highlight fraud or mistakes

### You've heard of the Emperor's New Clothes?

Because so few people really understand how Multicurrency really works in QuickBooks, they often steer clear of the *Exchange Gain or Loss* account. And dishonest employees can be tempted to take advantage of that. That's because they know that almost no one looks at the entries in that account, because they don't know what to make of them and why they're there.

This scenario is similar to the fairy tale of the Emperor's New Clothes, where no one wanted to admit they couldn't see the non-existent clothing the emperor thought he was wearing. With Multicurrency, no one wants to admit they don't know what the Exchange Gain or Loss account is displaying.

Over the years, I have seen more than my share of fraudulent transactions that were entered and "swept under the rug" by unscrupulous employees with access to QuickBooks, wishing to hide the fact that they're in essence stealing money from their employer. All they do is create bills and/or checks that affect the Exchange Gain or Loss account, rather than any other accounts on the Balance Sheet or Profit and Loss that people actually *do* explore.

## What transactions should you see in the Exchange Gain or Loss account?

Based on what we learned earlier, if we run an Account Quick-Report on the Exchange Gain or Loss account, there are very few transaction types that should appear there:

- Payment (i.e. Receive Payment on one or more foreign invoices)

*Ensure that this is for a foreign customer*

- Deposit (of received foreign payments or of foreign sales receipts)

*Drill down and look at the transaction, ensuring that it's only the change in the foreign currency value component that is affecting the Exchange Gain or Loss account*

- Bill Payment (i.e. Pay Bills for one or more foreign bills)

*Ensure that this is for a foreign vendor*

- General Journal (but only those that are Home Currency Adjustments)

*Drill down to open the general journal entries, to ensure that these are indeed Home Currency Adjustments*

Sometimes you will see other transactions such as bills and checks, with tiny amounts (such as a penny) appear on the Account QuickReport for the Exchange Gain or Loss account.That tiny amount is due to rounding on the exchange rates (this happens when there is a large amount of money being converted, and the exact conversion would require more decimal points in the exchange rate than QuickBooks can recognize), and that's just fine.

So take a look at the Account QuickReport. Drill down on Deposits and any other transactions just to make sure that the Exchange Gain or Loss account is just a tiny component of each entry.

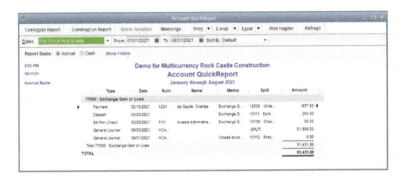

If you see any other entries besides the penny ones I mentioned, alert the authorities...someone is either attempting fraud or doesn't know what they're doing. Or both.

## Look at the exchange rates on transactions too: it may be fraud, or it may be lack of knowledge.

I have also seen my share of erroneous transactions that affect the Exchange Gain or Loss account.

Here's an example:

My client has entered a foreign invoice or bill, and never bothered to update the Currency List so that the exchange rate on the transaction was either old, inaccurate, or really wrong as it was at par with the home currency (i.e. 1).

And when the payment was made, they either kept the par exchange rate on the payment transaction, so no exchange gain or loss was recognized...or...in the interim they decided to start updating the exchange rates, and now the payment over-recognized the gain or loss component. That's because, depending on what the real exchange rate should have been on the bill or invoice (either the foreign currency is worth more or less than the home currency), the bill or invoice value in the home currency was over- or under-stated...and then the payment transaction with the exchange rates properly entered would understate the exchange gain or loss if the original transaction was overstated...or, it would overstate the exchange gain or loss if the original transaction was understated.

## What report can I run to see if the exchange rates are incorrect?

So the moral of this story is this:

For the report period (whether it's a month, a quarter, or a fiscal year, for example), go to **Reports > Accountant & Taxes > Journal**. Filter for one foreign currency, and add columns for the Currency and the Exchange Rate. Edit the Header to indicate which foreign currency is the filter and memorize it so that you can run the reports any time you like and do this for each foreign currency.

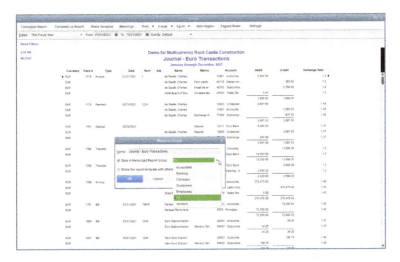

In fact, you can create an FX report group and memorize each foreign currency's report in there and then you can select **Reports > Process Multiple Reports** to run all the reports in the FX report group all at once.

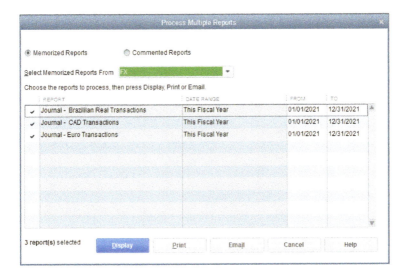

In each report, scroll down to review the exchange rate on each of that currency's transactions for reasonableness. If anything needs editing, go ahead and do that, assuming the reporting period is not closed with a closing date.

If you edit the exchange rate on a paid invoice, the payment transaction's foreign exchange component will change. This is also the case when editing an exchange rate on a paid bill.

# Chapter 22
# Foreign Currency: Miscellaneous Items to Consider

## Super Hard and Obscure Stuff:

### Finish This Module and You're an Absolute QuickBooks Multicurrency Expert

The previous modules and their lessons have taken you through QuickBooks Desktop's Multicurrency functionality, including all its nuances. But there are some unusual situations that you might encounter, and here you'll find the vast majority of them.

### Receive a Foreign Currency Payment on a Home Currency Invoice

If you have a home currency customer who owes you money, and they pay you in a foreign currency, QuickBooks Desktop will not allow you to deposit it into a foreign currency account. All it shows you is home currency accounts in which to deposit the home currency funds:

So use that Home Currency Clearing account to receive the payment as if it was in the home currency:

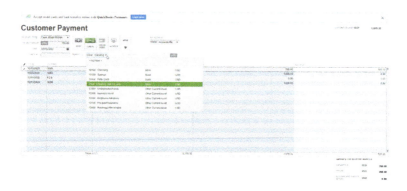

Then, transfer the funds from that Clearing account to the foreign currency account of your choice, overwriting the exchange rate for the rate that the bank is giving you, which of course will not be a great rate - they're taking their chunk of change here:

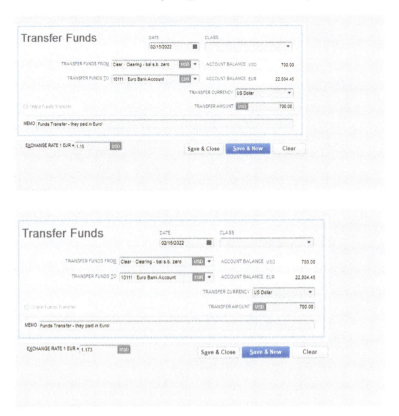

You'll likely get this Exchange Rate Changed screen, asking if you want this to be the new exchange rate for this currency on this date. Typically, you'll say No:

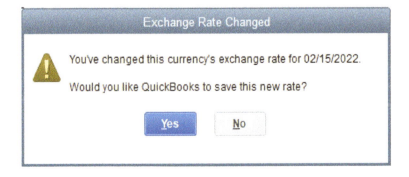

You'll know if you did things right if the Clearing account is at zero:

And of course, check the foreign bank account to make sure that the correct amount in that currency went into that bank.

This can be achieved by general journal entries as well, but it would require more than one entry because QBDT doesn't allow for more than one A/R or A/P account in a general journal entry. And it would make this process more difficult and prone to errors. This way is easier, believe me.

If they paid you in foreign currency and it went into a home currency bank account, you can receive the payment into the home currency bank BUT you'd need to see exactly how much went into the bank account in the home currency. Then receive the payment with that home currency value as if they paid you that in the home currency. There will likely be a small difference between the value of what they paid and the amount of the invoice, so you'd have to create an extra invoice if it's more, or a credit memo or a discount if it's less.

## Receive a Home Currency Payment on a Foreign Currency Invoice

If you have a foreign currency customer who owes you money, and they pay you in the home currency, QuickBooks Desktop allows you to deposit the funds into your home currency bank account.

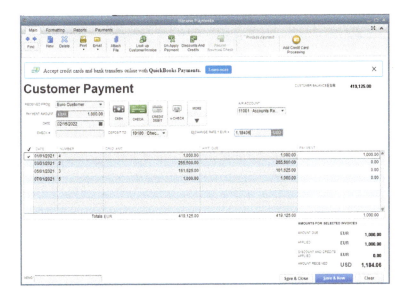

All you have to do is edit the exchange rate to reflect the lousy rate your bank is giving you:

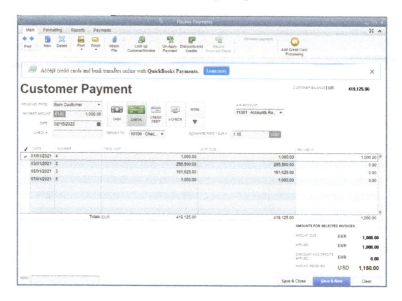

And then receive it directly into your home currency bank account, or receive the funds into Undeposited Funds and then deposit the money into the home currency bank account of your choice.

## Memorized Transactions in Foreign Currency

If you wish to memorize a foreign currency transaction, Quick-Books will not give you the option to automate it. That's because exchange rates in the future are unknown. So all you can do is either Add it to your reminders list or set it up as a "Do not remind me" memorized transaction that you can pick up at any time from the memorized transactions list and use.

## Post-dated Foreign Currency Transactions

If you wish to post-date a foreign currency transaction, Quick-Books will allow you to do it. However, it will assign the latest-dated exchange rate it has on file with that currency.

Let's create a check in the future to our Euro Vendor from our Home Currency Checking account. You can overwrite the exchange rate if you want to a rate you believe will take place in the future. That will update the rate in the future on the currency's exchange rate list.

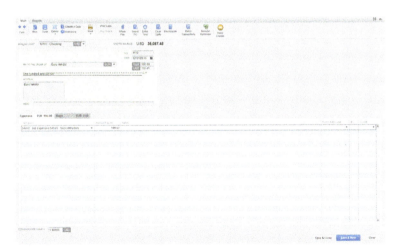

Or, if you are not happy with that exchange rate, you could go into the foreign currency listing and update a future exchange rate - QuickBooks Desktop *will* allow you to do this, even though it doesn't make sense - you don't have a crystal ball and you can't predict future exchange rates (if we did, we'd all be rich).

Then, when you enter the post-dated foreign currency transaction, QuickBooks will pick up the exchange rate you entered, assuming the date of your transaction is dated on or after the date of the future exchange rate you entered.

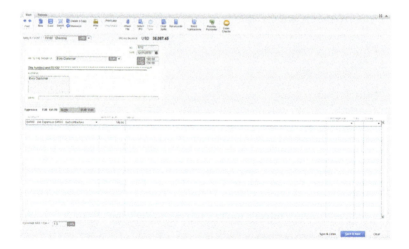

And, you can enter future exchange rates for a number of dates for each currency, if that helps you with your planning.

## Billable Time for Foreign Currency Customers

If you're tracking billable time, and you are trying to do this for foreign currency customers, here's what happens ...even if you've set up foreign pricing for this billable time's service item.

So we have this Generic Service item, with a selling price of $100.

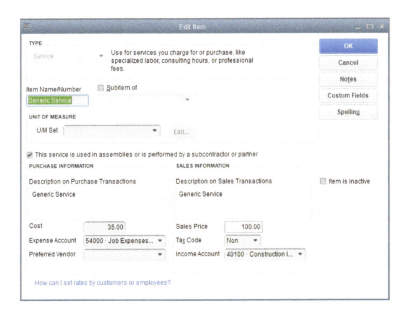

And I've set up a Per Item Price Level called "Euro Standard," giving this item a price of 90 euros regardless of the exchange rate with the home currency.

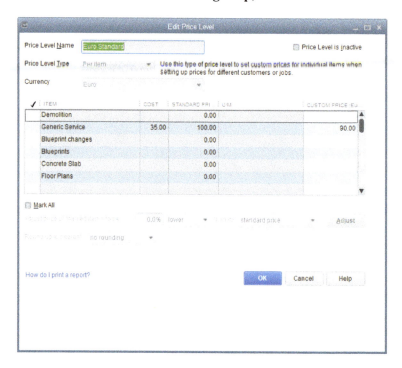

I've assigned this Euro Standard price level to my Euro Customer:

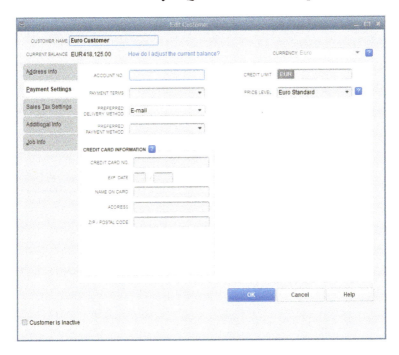

Now if I invoice that customer directly for this Generic Service item, the 90 euro price pops up on the invoice:

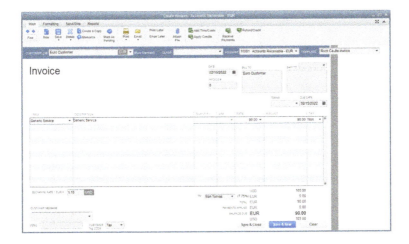

But what if I track billable time for this customer, using this Generic Service item?

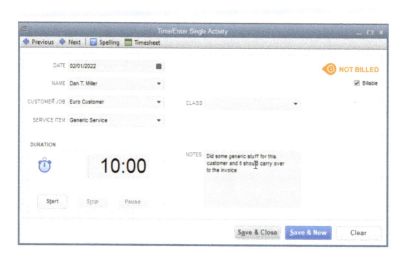

Now I want to invoice this customer the billable time, so I create an invoice and I'm prompted to add billable time/costs:

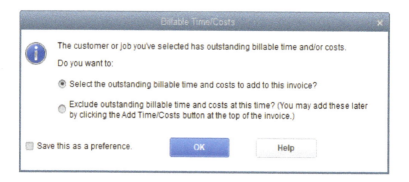

Notice that what shows up in the Time tab is the 10 hours but a different rate! Note that I've clicked on Options to choose to Enter a separate line on the invoice for each activity so I can see the description come over.

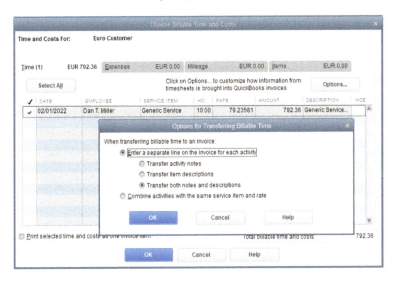

When you bring billable time over to an invoice, you'll see the home or domestic price for this item converted into the foreign price at whatever the prevailing exchange rate is on that date. In other words, the foreign pricing you've set up for this service item will not appear; instead, you'll see the domestic price you've set up for this item converted into the foreign currency at that day's exchange rate.

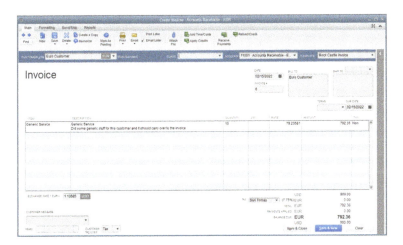

You'll need to overwrite this figure with the 90 euro from the price level.

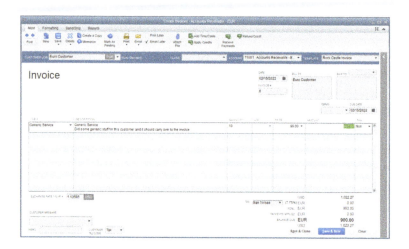

QuickBooks Desktop never fixed that.

## Billable Expenses in Foreign Currency

For **foreign customers**, here's a billable expense for 1,000 euro and it's for the Euro Customer:

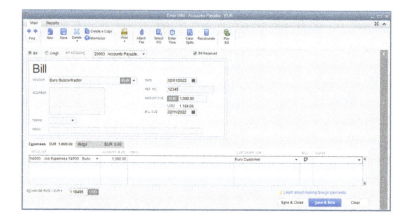

The Unbilled Costs by Job report shows this amount in the home currency:

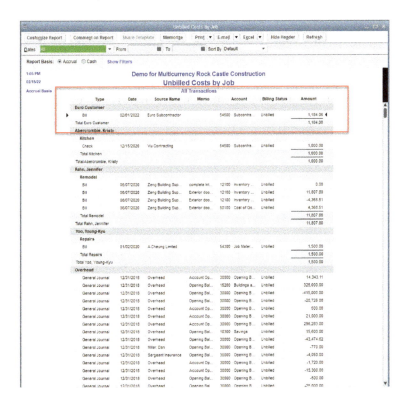

But I can customize this report to show the Foreign Amount and Currency as well:

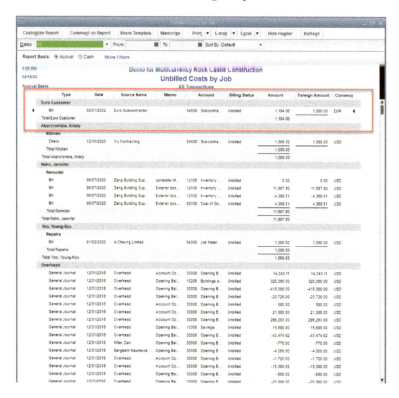

However, when I go to invoice this foreign customer today, it brings in a different amount based on what the billable expense was worth in the home currency on the date of the bill ($1,184.06), and then with the different exchange rate on the date of the invoice, it converts it back to the foreign currency. You might also get a warning that you're adding reimbursable expense items and the exchange rate cannot be changed once reimbursable expense items are added:

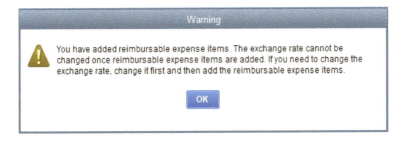

In this case, the amount that would be in the home currency appears converted back into a number of foreign currency units, being the euro.

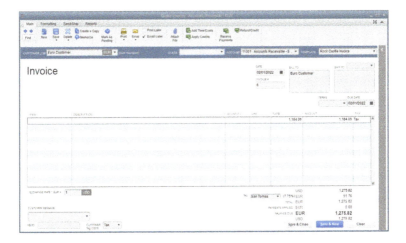

Then, you need to overwrite the amount in euro.

And if I have a foreign billable expense for a domestic or **home currency customer?**

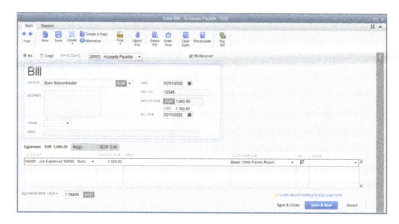

When I go to invoice that customer, the amount that comes over is the home currency value of the billable expense based on the exchange rate on the date of the bill. I may want to overwrite the home currency amount, but then again, if that's what it cost me on the bill, I may leave it as is - unless I want to mark it up.

## Assembly Items with Costs in Foreign Currency

Be aware that, since QuickBooks Desktop does not allow for price levels on costs, if you are using inventory assemblies and attempting to track the component costs in foreign currency, you will have to update the costs daily - or as often as you purchase the components.

QuickBooks Desktop is just not that sophisticated to track this.

## Tracking Fixed Assets and Mortgages in Foreign Currency

As you already know, the only accounts on the general ledger that can be assigned a foreign currency are banks, credit cards, accounts receivable (and its individual customers), and accounts payable (and its individual vendors).

Therefore, if you need to assign a foreign currency to a loan payable or mortgage account, you'll have to set it up as a credit card. And if you need to assign a foreign currency to an asset such as fixed assets or long term note receivable, you'll need to set it up as a bank account. It's not perfect, but it does work. Also, QuickBooks Online does offer the ability to assign a foreign currency to all balance sheet accounts other than equity.

Hypothetically, you could set up fixed assets and loans receivable as A/R and Mortgages and loans payable as A/P, but that would skew your receivables and payables reports, and also limit the types of transactions you can enter for these accounts. As many of you know, setting up accounts as A/R or A/P does bring with it some limitations.

QuickBooks Online behaves somewhat differently from Quick-Books Desktop when it comes to Multicurrency, and we're covering that in another book.

## Estimates in Foreign Currency

If you create a foreign currency estimate:

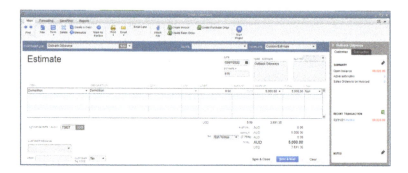

The default Estimates by Job report only displays it in its home currency equivalent:

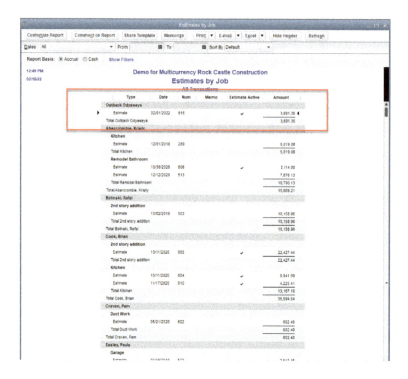

So you need to customize the report to show the foreign currency columns. Here, I'm doing a search in the Columns for the string "foreign" and checking off all of them:

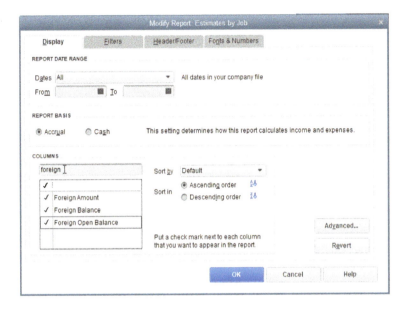

So the Estimates by Job report shows the amount in the foreign currency as well:

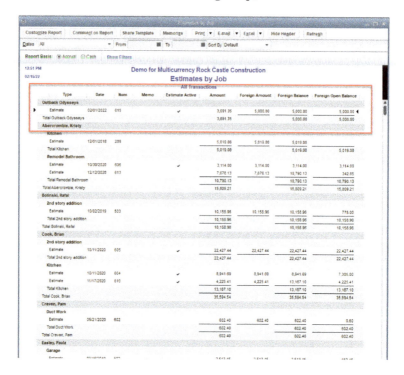

Now let's say I invoice partially from this estimate:

Now I have an invoice for 25% of the invoice but I'm changing the date of the invoice to a date with a vastly different exchange rate:

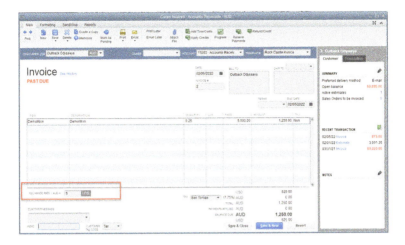

Now I re-display the customized Estimates by Job report:

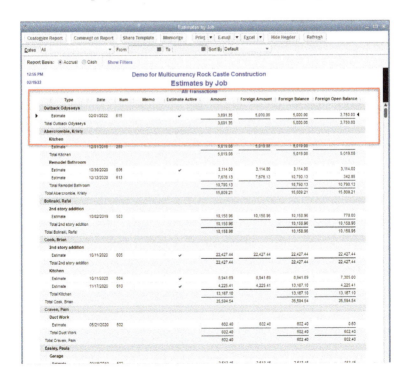

If I add the Open Balance column as well, I see the amount in the home currency as well:

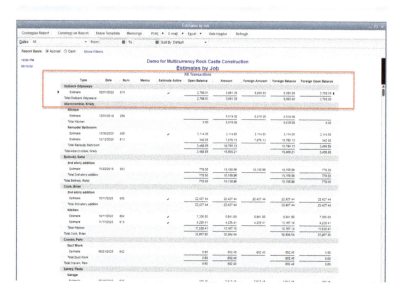

Note that, even with a different exchange rate on the invoice, the Open Balance figure is the same percentage of the original Amount figure as the Foreign Open Balance is of the Foreign Amount figure. There's no exchange gain or loss here.

## Customer or Vendor with More than One Currency

What if you have a large customer or vendor with whom you transact in more than one currency?

QuickBooks doesn't allow you to transact with a customer (such as invoices or sales receipts) or vendor (such as bills) in a currency other than the one that you've set up for them.

Therefore, in order to record different currency transactions, create a different customer or vendor for each currency. They have to be named differently, as QuickBooks doesn't allow more than one customer and/or vendor to have the same name.

So you might have Smithco (USD) as your US dollar customer and Smithco (CAD) as your Canadian dollar customer.

## Payment to Home Currency Payee from a Foreign Currency Bank

If you try and pay a home currency payee from a foreign currency bank, you'll get an error message telling you that the currency of the payee must match the currency of the bank account:

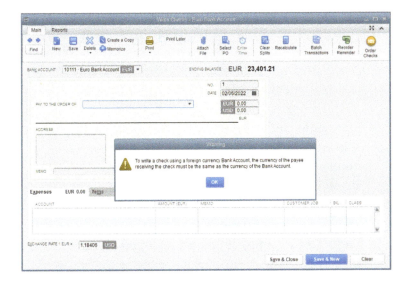

If that's the case, you can create a foreign currency payee that matches the currency of the source payment bank account. Just use the same account (such as "shareholder loan") that you would have used at the bottom of the check in the detail area in the Expenses tab.

## What if You Were Tracking Foreign Currencies Before Turning on Multicurrency?

I've seen many companies "track" foreign currency in Quick-Books without turning on the Multicurrency function. All this amounts to is basically labeling accounts as being in different currency, but the software actually tracks it as if it's in the home currency. So it's up to the accountant or bookkeeper to create regular revaluation transactions, usually monthly, to a separate account to track the foreign exchange difference between that foreign account's balance and what it would be worth if it were denominated in the home currency.

If that has been the case and now you want to turn on Multicurrency, here's what you need to do with what you've done already. Do this dated the day after the last tax filing date.

- Zero out foreign Balance Sheet accounts denominated in home currency, as well as outstanding foreign customer invoices, vendor bills that were denominated in home currency.
- Post all these zeroing out transactions to a clearing account on a particular date.
- Create new accounts, customers, and vendors in the real foreign currency with the proper exchange rates as of the same date.
- Re-create the balances in the foreign-denominated accounts and post to the same clearing account. There will be a difference, which is the net foreign exchange.
- Zero out the clearing account to the Exchange Gain/Loss account using a General Journal Entry

## What if You Want to Use Average Monthly Exchange Rates?

If you have a business in which you're advised to enter the mid-month or average exchange rate on all foreign currency transactions, by definition you have to enter them **after the fact**, when the exchange rates for the entire month are known.

If that's the case, calculate (or have your accountant provide you) the exchange rate you want to use for the entire month for each foreign currency. Then assign it to that currency dated the **first** day of the month and don't update the exchange rates for any other date in the month and certainly don't download the latest exchange rate! That means that you'll lose control over the exchange rates that pop up on transactions and you'll have to overwrite them all; this is prone to user error.

Do that for each month - just enter the average exchange rate as the rate for the first of each month.

Then any foreign currency transaction dated any date during each month will pick up the exchange rate from the first of that month because there are no other dates in the month that have an exchange rate.

## Now That This Book is Done and Dusted...

Thank you for reading this book.

We've covered just about every situation (normal and unusual) that you might encounter when dealing with multiple currencies in QuickBooks Desktop.

Sure, there are rare situations that may crop up that aren't covered by this book. But enumerating each of them would be overwhelming and meaningless for most students.

However, if you encounter one of these rare situations, you now likely have the skills and knowledge to figure out how to make QuickBooks Desktop work for you or your clients.

If there is a rare Multicurrency situation that you can't figure out, please reach out to Esther Friedberg Karp at esther@e-compubooks.com.

Now...go forth and *crush* QuickBooks Desktop Multicurrency!

# About the Author

Esther Friedberg Karp is an internationally-renowned trainer, writer, & speaker from Toronto, Canada, where she runs her QuickBooks consulting practice, EFK CompuBooks Inc.

Consistently in Insightful Accountant's Top 100 ProAdvisors, she's been named to the top 10 twice. She is a QuickBooks ProAdvisor in three countries (Canada, the U.S., and the U.K.) and the International edition of QuickBooks Online, has spoken and appeared around the world, and has written countless articles for Intuit Global.

Esther has been named one of the Top 50 Women in Accounting, a Top 10 Influencer in the Canadian Bookkeeping World, and is a repeat nominee for the RBC Canadian Women's Entrepreneur Awards. She counts among her clients many international companies, as well as accounting professionals seeking her out on behalf of their own clients for her expertise in multicurrency and various countries' editions of QuickBooks Desktop and Online.

Esther has spoken, written, and trained on the multicurrency functions in QuickBooks Desktop and Online for clients of all sizes and industries, and is considered to be one of the world's leading experts on Multicurrency and QuickBooks.

Website: www.e-compubooks.com

facebook.com/EFKCompuBooks

twitter.com/estherfriedberg

linkedin.com/in/estherfriedbergkarp